Words out there

Women Poets in Atlantic Canada

Edited by Jeanette Lynes
Foreword by Gwendolyn Davies

Roseway Publishing
Lockeport, Nova Scotia

Roseway Publishing gratefully acknowledges the support of the Nova Scotia Department of Education, Cultural Affairs Division, and the Canada Council.

Cover collage (mixed media): *To Let Go* by Susan Wood
Cover and book design: Brenda Conroy
Proofreading: Michèle Raymond
Printed and bound in Canada by
Hignell Printing, Winnipeg, MB

Published by Roseway Publishing Co. Ltd.
Lockeport, Nova Scotia B0T 1L0
phone/fax (902) 656-2223
email ktudor@atcon.com
www.outdoorns.com/~roseway

Canadian Cataloguing in Publication Data
Main entry under title:
Words out there: women poets in Atlantic Canada

ISBN 1-896496-09-1

1. Canadian poetry (English) — Women authors. ★ 2. Canadian poetry (English (Atlantic provinces. ★ 3. Canadian poetry (English) — 20th century.★ I. Lynes, Jeanette. II. Davies, Gwendolyn.

PS8283.W6W68 1999   C811'.5408'09287 C99-950085-6
PR9195.3.W68 1999

for Collette and Ian

Contents

The Poets

Foreword

What is overwhelming for the first-time reader of these twenty-three Atlantic women poets is the strength, the power, of their "words out there." They have spoken, as Heather Browne Prince has put it, to break the silence. And out of that silence, out of "words that swivel in my head" (Fitch), have come poems that speak of place, time, memory, community, spirituality, and the process of craft and creativity.

The words reverberate. But they reverberate with an astonishing thread of commonality. Disparate as these poets are in background, cultural experience, and even physical geography, they are all preoccupied with the sound of voices. They meditate on the flattening out of sound (MacLeod), the punctuation of words by silence (Prince), the orality and musicality of language (Fitch), the energy of idiom (Dalton), the speech rhythms of the elderly (Pierce), the voicing of love (Rita Joe), and the intoning of names (Tynes). "The powerful thing," notes Carole Langille, "is to listen to the voices."

In the 1780s, Nova Scotian poet, Deborah How Cottnam ("Portia"), taught her female students in Saint John and Halifax to use their samplers as a form of alternate text for poetic expression. Forty-five years later, her great granddaughter, the poet Griselda Tonge of Windsor, Nova Scotia, paid tribute to the influence of "Portia's hallow'd lyre" as she invoked the powers of literary continuity that linked one generation of female voices to the next.

The continuity of voices that Griselda Tonge envisaged finds fruition in the poems and interviews of the twenty-three Atlantic women poets published in this collection. Whether hanging laundry with "mother's hands" (Hull), drawing on "minds" that "are museums" (Simpson), or "writing" as "a kind of seeing" (Davies), these poets emerge under the sensitive interviewing and editing of Jeanette Lynes as collectively embarked on a journey "to tell the truth. To try to see beyond repression, prejudice, ideological limitations. To bear witness to our time and place. But also, to go forward into the dark, to imagine a new mythos, to find a new field where we can create" (Pyrcz).

Gwendolyn Davies
Acadia University, Wolfville, Nova Scotia

Introduction

There are words out there
that will light up the tomb.
         — *Carole Langille*

Some years ago, Elizabeth Bishop wrote a poem about taking a journey by bus. In this poem, entitled "The Moose," the bus rumbles through New Brunswick and as night falls, its passengers do what passengers do. Some doze off. Others talk. The poet-traveller listens to their words in the darkness, to the voices "talking, in Eternity." Whole worlds emerge from these words suspended in air, then caught in the lines of the poem.

This book is about words shining in the darkness. In their various ways, these twenty-three women poets from Canada's eastern provinces carry forward the act of listening to the voices. Like Elizabeth Bishop's traveller, these poets remain vigilant, alert, on their journeys into various landscapes. These landscapes are not determined by regional boundaries; nor are they defined exclusively by geography. Ancestry and the historical dimensions of place often play an equally important role.

The first section of *Words Out There* brings together work by contemporary women poets in Atlantic Canada. The second section documents, in interviews, the poets' reflections on their craft. The poetry of the book's first part and the poetics of its second section, it is hoped, complement each other. The reader will find considerable variety in these pages. The poets represent a diverse group of writers who bring to their craft a broad range of influences. The poets come from different backgrounds, reflecting the cultural multiplicity of Atlantic Canada. Despite their varied backgrounds and distinct voices, they share with each other and with all poets a passionate engagement with language and place. For these writers, poetry is a way of being, a way of situating themselves in the world in both a local and global sense. These poets describe the act of writing in various ways. For some, writing poetry is "spiritual practice." For others, writing is a way of reclaiming self, reclaiming culture, reclaiming place. Over and over, the poems and dialogues in these pages attest to the affirming power of words.

Words Out There features both established and emerging poets.

All the writers, including the "emerging" ones, have published a substantial body of poetry. Many have won literary awards. Several have worked in the theatre; some are also visual artists. A number of these writers have published fiction.

The interviews took place between September 1997 and March 1999. Most were recorded on tape and then transcribed, but several were conducted by email, fax, and letters. Some transcriptions were supplemented by email exchanges. The interviews took place in living rooms, hotel rooms, lounges, on university campuses, a front porch, and in a Frenchy's Used Clothing store.

Only so much can be held between the covers of a book. This book is no exception. It offers a partial, rather than exhaustive, picture of contemporary women's poetry in Atlantic Canada. There are other strong poets in the country's eastern provinces. To make a list only creates more exclusions. However, some of these poets are mentioned in the interviews, and in that sense, are present. Unfortunately, I was unable to contact Kay Smith for an interview.

Words Out There could not have existed without the support of many people. Making this book has been such a rewarding journey because of the poets themselves, and I would like to thank them for their generosity and patience. I am also very grateful to Kathleen Tudor at Roseway Publishing. The many months of hard work Brenda Conroy put into the design of this book will always be appreciated. Special thanks to Gwendolyn Davies, Collette Saunders, Ian Colford, and Anne Simpson. Carole Langille provided the inspiration for the title. Thanks to Susan Wood for allowing us to use her collage for the cover. Richard Lemm and Sheree Fitch made helpful suggestions during the early stages of the book. The Writers' Federation of Nova Scotia and The Writers' Federation of New Brunswick provided valuable contact information. Bruce Campbell, Brian Bartlett, Christy Ann Conlin, Lorna Crozier, Robin DeLorey, Marie Gillis, P.K. Page, and Michèle Raymond,were helpful in the final phase. Mary McGillivray provided encouragement throughout this project. And as always, many thanks to David Lynes, for everything.

I am grateful to Lakehead University for providing a sabbatical leave from 1997-98 so that this project could be undertaken. Mount Saint Vincent University provided office space and professional affiliation during fall 1997; special thanks to Susan Drain.

Jeanette Lynes
Antigonish, Nova Scotia

Acknowledgements

The Poems:

Some of the poems first appeared in the following publications:

Maxine Tynes' "Let There Be Sex" in her book *The Door of My Heart;*" Don't Give Me Looks" in her book *Woman Talking Woman.*

Lesley-Anne Bourne's "The Story of Pears" in her book *The Story of Pears;* "Arctic Faces" in her book *Field Day.*

Lynn Davies' "Tonight the Violent Wind" in *Contemporary Verse II;*" Briefly, Abelard Tries to Understand" in *Grain.*

Regina Coupar's "legacy" and "sophia rising" in her book *Light Among the Shadows.*

Margaret McLeod's "No Wolves, I Tell You" in *Fiddlehead;* "Ghostchild" in *Event* and *The Windhorse Reader: Choice Poems of '93.*

The Poets:

Excerpts from some of the interviews first appeared in *Pottersfield Portfolio,* Volume 18, Number 3, Spring 1998.

The Poems

Carole Langille

What Poems Cost

I go where poems are.
In the market? At the lecture?
Through the book's long chapter?

If they're not there I leave,
so I can locate, like a magnet
sound's trigger. What I need

may be overheard
when stones fall into water
or sap bleeds.

During the day,
like the call to prayer,
I forgive. I honour. Or try.

You can't be this
without this.
Lie low. But care

for what begs care.
You need a lot of time
humbly to address yourself.

Like a stream filled with rocks and weeds,
but fast moving, I am pulled
by something deep in the earth.

Much of what I do,
so much dreaming, I conceal.
But there's a wish

to reveal as well. This is
the low, steady song
of having lost or having won

what,
by God's law,
can't be wagered.

There's strong desire.
And pride?
"That's a lust in man no charm can tame."

The prize,
to cherish what cannot be forced.
This is the day's wage.

To give thanks to crows
when they alight with their omens
in the fields, by an open gate.

And for the hour
hope leaps
off the printed page.

There are words out there
that will light up the tomb.
Let us pull down every weight.

Not in the Warm Earth

This is where we come
to find our parents.
In the fine cloth. In the neat hand. Did you
make this for me, mother? Are you
proud Father, though I didn't
hit the ball, though I didn't
go to meetings?
I lived mostly in my dreams. Remember,
I would go into the yard, my bike
a horse. I'd race. I'd vault
fences. By the time I got home,
I'd crossed the border,
was in my late thirties, children
holding both my hands.
New lock on an old door.

This is where we find our parents,
white water rafting down the rapids
in the same boat we're in.
But it tips, it turns over.
I can't save them.

In the middle of the night
they wake me. They say I've made mistake
after mistake. They're worried.
I get up. Heat milk. Tell them
I visit often. Am still touched
by incandescent moments
of their great caring, their heroic endeavours.
I know how hard it was to live
in that house. In that life. "But,
Mother it's late. Father, you're dead, it's time
you were asleep. When you *do* visit
you don't have to rattle the doors,
I'll be listening. Knock gently. Tell me
why have you come. What can I give you?

M. Travis Lane

Elegy

There, on the tarmac, where they fixed
the ice-heaves after Easter,
where a wreath
of plastic roses and dried leaves,
frayed ribbons fading, lies,
you
    (sound of a snowflake on the sea)
fell —

where the bullet nicked
concrete.

The city is paved with invisible blood.
We, who have grown vague-headed, grey,
could have spoken your name like a poem,
once.

What is the purpose of poetry
when what we want to remember
we forget?
You, like a sand-grain in a storm,
snow-splinter —

Earth drains from the meadows of the stars
hallucinogenic skeins,
words without letters, and numbers without signs,
silences deeper than silences.

You, too, once burned.

Rains have washed the sidewalks clean.
Hard weathers have dissolved
even the scowls of the sculptured saints,
and numbed the pierced cathedrals.
Where the trees
nailed sky a bitter snow
has hung its funereal wedding cake.
The party is over. The guests have gone.

I would bring you something:
a tiny box
of birthday candles, pink and small
as the fingers of mice, a poetry
which will not stand unaided where you stood,
or where you fell.

Or perhaps it was somewhere else you fell.
Under the children's graveled swings?
Or there, where the students rack their bikes?
Or that rope-laundried balcony?
It was somewhere, there, when the sun came out
just briefly. You blazed.
Yes, it was that
we remember. Yes,
it was those
white scarves
they tied over your eyes to blind themselves.

It was here, or somewhere else,
perhaps. Perhaps in the woods,
ducking among the tree trunks like a gaunt
wolf shadow, where a twig
snaps, or quick
life — see where the bullet chipped
bark —

Suburbs of snow and vacant lots
where mouse paths blur,
where the drifts enshroud
the barbed-wire tangles, the steel snares,
the emptied cartridge cases, where the thin
junk-headed aspens grow, weeds that come up
after fire —
slag heaps of cinders, or oyster shells,
cities and histories erased —

Look for the semi-private round
of the plains teepee,
or the blackened turf
where the smoky longhouse hunched, or where
a hunter made camp and gathered brush
for one night only —
tracks of a city
that in my hands
crumbles like silt on a snowy page.

Nothing stays written.

The hills move into the darknesses.
Trees,
like exhalations from the mass
grave pits below them, wither, fade.

Look under the graying tentacles
of roots, of clay, of dripping stone.
Look to the deepest burrows of a mine
shored by the rotting buttresses
of an ignored religion. There,
your name falls like a water drop
to a hidden pool —

    eye has not seen
    nor ear has heard —

Into that utter namelessness
we, too,
return.

Mary Dalton

Oldfella and Mr. Subaru

So a tourist sees an old man dragging a tree from the
    woods. And he asks, "What's that you've got there?"
The old man says, "A starrigan."
The tourist, puzzled, "How do you spell that?"
The old man replies, "Well, in the summer I spells en out on
    me back and in winter I spells en out with me 'ars."
                              — Newfie joke

    The people were saying no two were e'er wed
    But one had a sorrow that never was said.
                    "She Moved Through the Fair"

So it's the Great Divide again.
So let's walk over the Great Big Joke again.
It's the tourist —
It's always the tourist —
Picture him, sleek, with his Tilley hat,
His rosy cheeks, his mutual funds,
His fanny-pack, his good intentions,
His Subaru.
So he sees this Oldfella.
Y'know — the generic Newfoundlander.
Hauling a dead tree out of the woods.
Already it's funny;
You can feel your belly begin to lift.
You're geared for a tasty fat laugh.
A rib-sticking Jiggs Dinner of a laugh.
The Oldfella. The dead tree. Mr. Earnest Subaru.
So the tourist asks, not
Knowing a dead tree from a hole in the ground,
"What's that you've got?"
And the Oldfella, well-used

To the weird questions of the simple folk from away,
And unfailingly courteous to boot,
And ever willing to stand and chat
While dragging wood from the woods —
Such is the pace of life for oldfellas in the Land of Funnytalk —
The Oldfella says,
"A starrigan."
And Mr. Subaru, fiddling with his camera,
"Oh, what's that?"
He knows how to draw the folk out.
No flies on him.
And the Oldfella wants to help,
To break the dark, to shed the light.
"A var," he says. "A var."
"How do you spell that?"
Home to the dictionary —
Or is there one in the fanny-pack?
Ah, thinks Oldfella, an enquiry about method —
The relentless *How* that enthralls himself
As it did his mother and his mother's mother —
Ah, now, here's a fella interested in the way of it —
Perhaps they'll hit it off after all.
"Well in summer I spells en out
On me back and in winter I spells
En out with me 'ars."
So the Great Big Joke leaves them there.
Mr. S. agape, yes, mouth open wide —
And Oldfella's heart sinking, yea, into the lower
Regions of his stomach, foiled yet again,
Thwarted from what had looked,
For a second, to become a talk with some sense in it.
Mr. S., shaking his head (and his hat), makes his way on,
Christian with his burden,
Bemused by the brutish babble,
(That's good, he thinks,
Jots it in his field book:
Brutish babble;
The scatalogical wordings
Of these salty primitives;

Next to the pasted-in
Ad from Holiday
Inn and Air Canada: Earn
Points While You Sleep.)
Somewhere a horse scratches
Its behind and laughs, laughs.
Neighs roar down the sky,
Split it, our Great Divide

Maiden Vein

So you'd trick death,
Gallivant out to sail in, jack-easy?
Know the signs; keep a keen eye.
If you've a mind to flout storms
And the jaws of fierce weather,
Scan the maiden vein:
Gale or soft breeze —
It'll prance out at dawn
From where the maiden vein
In the night sky spills its silver.
And you a lamb to the slaughter
Or king of the cod.

Liliane Welch

Monet's Prayer at Rouen

Fencing with the cathedral's façade
he composed air into a cello
symphony which played only in colour.

Drunk with stone, he painted
the load of that world,
quarried salvation on his canvas.

Saints kneeled on the Gothic arches
while he was threatened with
expulsion from his workshop.

Swollen thumb locked in his palette,
eyes steady, heart wide open
as a rose window, a grand portal,

the lone, bearded wild man prayed.

Marsilio Casotti and His Bride Faustina

Lorenzo Lotto Exhibition, Paris 1998

Above the young couple
the Cupid is musing
I'll place this yoke
on their shoulders. They must
learn to endure each other.
Celebrate hard times!
I wonder if
Marsilio thinks:

"She'll be faithful even
though she's the most beautiful
maiden of Bergamo. But can
the cautious pleasures
of marriage reach ecstasy
without brooding on
other loves?"

The Cupid glances at Faustina.
Holding out her finger
to become wife,
she's not submissive,
and her espresso eyes reflect
a Frenchman, absorbed in lust,
who just then stares at her.

Maxine Tynes

Let There Be Sex
Let There Be Love
Let There Be Power
Let There Be Lies

And so to the shouting stage
come these two who are all of us
to parade and to inventory
their past and their present selves
to be all and nothing at all
to themselves
to each the other
to reveal and to dissemble
and to construct and reconstruct
the tract and the tissue of
tears and the truth

and so we are the chorus of
this everyman
this everywoman

we/they resurrect and bury
the life/the work they once shared
and dared to make bold and malleable
in the face of power and of eros

this Anita and this Clarence
this woman and this man
this Pygmalion and this Galatea
this Tristan and this Isolde
this Sampson and this Delilah
this woman and this man

when sex becomes love
when love becomes power

when power becomes a lie
when the Fourth Estate is
the tribunal and the crucible

when the past is the present
when the moment is made
when the word is made omnipotent

ten years ago
the currency and
the climate of sex
        of love
        of power
was an open market
a thrusting sea
for the ebb and flow of
women and men
astride that tide of
thrust and parry
the powerplay of climbing
of using and leading
and following
of mentor and of protegée

when the hand that rocked
the status quo
straightened a tie
felt a thigh
smoothed a skirt
shuffled a flirtatious glance or word
or whispered into the stacked deck of
stock reports, lies, stats and spreadsheets

Oh my libido as I climb
Oh my libido as I mentor
Oh my libido as I sit at your feet
Oh my libido as I loosen my tie

Oh my libido as I seek promotion
Oh my libido as I promote you
Oh my libido as I lead the way

Oh my libido as you follow
Oh my libido as the curtain rises
on the powerplay

Oh my libido as we invent/reinvent
assume roles in the powerplay

Oh my libido as I/we/you
invent and reinvent the script
this language of sex
        of love
        of power
        of the future lie

Oh my libido as first you, then I
am in turn, a Caesar for the other
and then, we each, in turn
become that unknown factor in the equation

Who is Caesar?
Who is Brutus?
Et tu, Clarence?
Et tu, Anita?

We become a willing and
hungry chorus for you
our appetite for promise
matched only by your
ready stream of lies and dated panache

from Washington to the world
we tuned in
turned dials
compared notes

held back tears
shed tears
called friends and made revelations
called friends and made amends
turned our bedrooms and

our boardrooms into
some collective shouting stage

tore the names of old lovers out
of old datebooks
held them up to the light
flushed the torn up bits away.

Don't Give Me Looks

Don't give me looks that put me in my place
that open my mail
that smell me coming and going, and see me everywhere.
Don't give me looks made of plastic smiles
reserved for co-workers who rush past
on a wave of caffeine and nicotine,
letting 'How are you?' drift and hang in the air.
You say, 'Fine!' neither hearing nor meaning it.
Don't give me those looks.
Don't give me looks full of hell and damn
and who cares? who cares?
that flap on the line like clothes in the wind
that ring and ring like a telephone in an empty room
that flicker white and snowy, like the telly at midnight
that are snowblind in August
that are full of all the rest of the world
and not me.

Rita Joe

Kuntewe'wey Wikwom (Stone Wigwam)

My stone wikwom may not reach the sky
It will be there for you to learn
I was my own.
Though I spoke in two
Sometimes three
As long as it shows.

———————————

I will never be gone
The shade behind the toil
Always like the wikwom ...

Lnasku'k (Wampum)

The Word of Truth

Wampum was used by my people the Mi'kmaq
In the Northeastern part of North America
In a way of recording messages, sending them.
It consisted of purple and white beads
from the shell of quahog, clams.
The beads were strung in strands
Or woven into belts.
Like those made on bead-looms of today.
The design on beaded string made the messages remembered.
By the carrier of the wampum, Putu's
Lnapsku's were sacred to the native.
The word of truth in them.

It was used to maintain or terminate political relations.
Among the Mi'kmaq and other aboriginal nations.
Alliances, peace agreements
And things of mutual interest,
To hold family life, marriage proposals
To show positions of power to the nation.
To perform ceremonials.
To show alliances, agreements
To a leader of a country he wanted as allies.

Out of respect for our way
I suggest a leader send a wampum to all of us.
I teach what it signifies, honor.

Lesley-Anne Bourne

The Story of Pears

This afternoon under
the pear trees, I thought

without you, I have
whatever I like.

No. As many pears as
I'd like? Did we say

something about love
that mattered? The breeze

stared up
through the leaves

and your hands
stopped. Chances

are you don't remember —
but then how could you

touch a pear, the skin so ripe
where the stem breaks,

the sunlight there
in the woods, how could you

know how true
and round in your palm

the pear felt?

Arctic Faces

"Arctic faces infant time bomb"
  — *The Globe and Mail*, headline, July 13, 1994

Today my sister is moving
across the country — I
supervise. Already
she's relocated, switched
ocean gables for lakeside
bungalow windows facing
west. Most beautiful
sunsets in the world said the ad

the only day it ran.
Out here the ancient porch surrounds
the bomb I expect
once she's gone. White boards
line up the faraway summers we were
cottage mermaids, woodland savages
climbing cliffs at the age

some girls give birth
in the Arctic. Hard to read
The Globe in the maritime
breeze on the porch that's my sister's
one more day. She lives on
Baffin Island I tell myself so
the real distance shrinks — if I squint,
the ocean wrinkles into lake

and smells like water she
learned to dive in
while I waited on the dock
to grow up, afraid
she'd gone for good. Underwater
holding her breath longer
than my father or anyone she raced
after dinner. From wooden chairs

we scanned the middle of the lake
where she'd surface, loon
silhouetted at dusk.
The movers want to know
what she looks like,
this woman provinces away.
They glimpse in her closet

silky things and in cupboards
blue dishes already wrapped.
The men say I look like her
arctic face as they pack
picture frames. Please see
Inuit, page three, it says. Please
come back, I didn't cry this morning

phoning to say the movers
arrived and are handsome
by the way, are you sure
you want to leave here?
That was before the guy shattered
his truck window
on the driveway tree.
Maybe the explosion

was as bad
as it gets hour by hour,
the house, barer than the tundra
I imagine, hardwood floors the colour of
sand at the edge
of the cold lake we waded,
locking hands in case
someone turned back.

Carmelita McGrath

Reclining

When you are young and you learn a word
you want to lie down in it.
Reclining–its languid shape
suggested to me chaise
and other things we didn't have to sit on.
I had an arm tanned and curved
that ended in a thin brown hand
that wanted to drape itself, reclining
on the curve of the old settee
in the house where I lived briefly as comfort child,
antidote to my grandfather's lingering death.
Horsehair, that settee, or straw;
leather its cover or oilcloth
and the curve of its back a harp or heart.
First nights in the house,
the present did not seem
so distant from the past.
Granda regaled us with storms and squirting squid,
dories tossed in the air on the big water, a great
sea-drama where a boy tore out and ate a live fish's heart
and was cured of seasickness forever. Then the salt,
the gales, misleading fogs played treachery.
Words mangled; my grandfather's stories dissolved
into a storm that went on and on.
In the back room his bed tossed like a skiff
and he called for an end
even if it meant going under.
Those nights of pain I was away upstairs
in jungles where jaguars hid in emerald trees,
where a Pope expired relentlessly in a painting
and the weird sisters, hag and hag, laid
their bodies against mine and sucked my breath.
I was twelve then; one night I ran away
to home. They sent my younger sister in my stead.
After, I thought of reclining in the parlour

on the old settee but felt
the weight of my grandfather's death press on me.
It was where they waked him, in that corner
where I'd imagined myself sprawled
reading stories in a leafy light.
But his afterimage clung there, as if the air
had photographed him reclining chill and quiet.

Booman

Beware the shadowy booman in the evening garden,
a spectre from the years the grass grew high
as houses. Beware the moment when light is unsure.
There he'll be waiting,
all smoke and shadow and shimmer-shape.
With the crook of his finger, he'll beckon you over
'cross the crimped summer hay he'll call you, say
"My, you're after getting some nice fat legs.
My, what a grand big girl."
Once he appeared in a cellar door;
he was not there a second before.
His face wavered in the heat haze
and it was not night, but the burnished
centre of an August day.
I caught his gaze upon my scrawny shape
like a small, chill wind from nowhere,
rising and teasing and falling,
all in a moment, and gone.
The booman waited, found me late
at night on a city street
where trees were thick and crowds thin,
tried to frig me, frighten me
but I got away with loud curses,
the pump of my grand girl's legs. I still expect him
some nights on some streets
where the dark lies heavy and sweet and deep
as the grass where I first found him.
The best protection is to never discount him.

Heather Browne Prince

The Practice of Walking

It is this habit of walking
which shapes and steadies.
This practice whereby

feet and spine marry
the ground-swell of hummocks,
the descent of springs,

and the rock-lift of diorite
into the mind. It is this;

not the treading pump and hiss
of a school bus, braking.

A Man, His Old Sweater

Love unscrews the electric light bulbs,
sits you down in the dark. Living with ghosts
I've called out familiar names
in the shower stall. Crouched. The water pulsing;
I could go on. But let me tell you this;

I woke up one morning, recognized the furniture
as my own, my coffee table, that old Jezebel.
I tried on my wind breaker, it fit.
I hung it on the hook, and it shook a little,
so happy to be back. Next thing

I'm looking for an old jersey, bright wool,
old friend. Then I'm putting on the kettle.
I can't believe it yet.
It's true: the longest journey
I ever took was the one leading back to here.

Agnes Walsh

Homecoming to the End

That way he had of looking over his glasses at me
when I tried to say something matter-of-fact,
But knew I wasn't pulling it off.
He wouldn't say anything — would never answer right away,
just go back to his paper
and say it to the print, matter-of-fact.

I told him I was going to marry a sailor
and go away. He said: "Go away?
To where you know no one?"
That stopped me, made me lonely
Before I'd made the steady plans.
"It's your life, and you can always change
your mind," he said.
He made it difficult to rebel.

Years later, he rowed us across Southeast Arm.
With the sail up, the air felt softer on the skin,
the mind relaxed into a carefree sinking.
The open canvas flapped in the wind,
billowing out like a blossoming magnolia.
As he coasted us in, I trailed my hand through the water.
Then the *plunk, plunk* of each oar
hauled over, and placed inside the boat.

Dad cut off a thumb-size slice of tobacco.
"You can row back," he said, "if the tide is right.
If not, I'll take her, or we can wait 'til the tide turns."

I thought, how odd for him — his daughter gone away
and come back with a southern accent.
I remembered that line from *Gone With The Wind,*
where the black servant says, "I don't know nothin'
'bout birthin' no babies, Miss Charlotte."
I'd change that around to, "I don't know nothin'
'bout rowin' no dory, Daddy."
But he wouldn't get the joke — besides, we never joked.
Joke was an American word, like cookie, and divorce.

I sat transcribing ballads from cassette tape to page.
He leaned into the doorjamb of my bedroom,
listening to the songs where he knew the people
who had died in gales, or the sly youths
who had gotten away with something.
I'd say, "What's that, Dad? What's he saying?"
He'd look over his glasses at the machine:
"Clamped ahold to" or "Two-buckle spring in your knee,"
he'd say, a grin spreading into silent memory.
I'd imagine him leaning on a wall at a dance,
waiting to make sure he'd pick the right girl to ask.
Mom said, "Your father would wait 'til the end of the night
to ask for a dance, right when you'd thought
he never cared for you. A hard man to figure out."

But he was never hard. No. His curse word was "Judas."
His temperament even, his pace full and steady.
At his wake, a man took my hand and said,

"Your father wasn't a man you prayed for, but prayed to."
I turned away. I didn't want him made into a saint,
a man unreachable. I wanted his prejudices, his blind
church-going to meet my sinful life of drinking and manizing.
I wouldn't let him get away from me that easy.
He wouldn't rise at the right hand of anyone.

So I lay in his bed the night he was buried,
remembering his hand in mine, us going for ice cream.
Mom banged on the door: "Come out, you'll drive your nerves bad.
Come out and join the party for your father."
But I lay there surrounded by his few clothes hanging,
the smell of Beaver plug, the crucifix,
the blurred and moving Blessed Virgin dissolving into the Bleeding Heart.
I lay with his words and stories — ships hove into rocks,
St. Pierre wine in wooden casks, the whaling factory in Rose au Rue,
words I clung to, knowing his passing took away a world.

In the morning, before dawn, a light touch on my head,
a blur of white mist in the room, the faraway words trailing off:
"Get up, now, and let me rest. Go on and help your mother, now."
I threw back the blanket and stumbled into the grey light of day.

Sheree Fitch

This body is growing a person inside

Baby is a trick word.
To say you're going to have a baby
is actually impossible. You give birth.
But you never own.
You never *have.*

To say baby is to say cherub cheeks and dimpled wrists
Warm snuggle bunny baby bundle
Maybe we do hear a faint echo of crying and the smell of baby shit
But both are sweet to the ear and nose in conception.
The word baby *is* a concept.

What if everyone said instead
This body is growing a person inside
Picture that chalky fish on the ultrasound screen as
Infant, toddler, kid and adolescent
Finally a grown person with mortgage bills
No job and child support to pay
Picture inside you a temper tantrum
A feisty three year old scribbling on the walls
A face full of acne
A lip being stitched
A weeping teenager heartbroken for the first time
A doorslamming adolescent
Picture yourself inside yourself for a second.
(Now there's a terrifying thought)

What if, for a full nine months you see baby
As an old person with false teeth, pleated face
Halitosis, osteoporosis and a bruised heart?

Much wiser to say instead:
This body is growing a person inside
Maybe then, you will be better prepared
When Baby stands before you
Framed in the arch of a doorway
Waving good-bye with a promise to call
A baby you can no longer hold
                   no longer rock
                   no longer make it better for
Just watch instead
As they go out into a world
That most days
is just not good enough
For any baby you might dare to call your own.

To Begin With: Why I Left Earth & Other Confessions

One night walking home in a freezing rain that pricks the skin like shards of asbestos I looked up at the moon. It seemed to me to be some golden eyebrow raised above the earth. Then, as if I were watching some sort of photo simulation fastforwarding the phases of the lunar cycle the moon ballooned out before me becoming some helium filled cycloptic eye that blinked once then bellowed:

-How do you all still have gall enough to call yourselves a human planet?

It was not an angry voice, more a sandpaper whisper that reminded me of dead leaves as they cartwheel on down dusty roads a sound that makes even your bones lonely and your throat close.

A cabbie was driving past & I heard tin whistles and singing like wind chimes.

Hypnotized, I held my face up to the sky until the rain bit through my cheekbone & I wondered if miniature daggers of rain on nights like this could stab deeply enough to make one bleed so I held my hand to my cheek clutched my bag of milk and bread in the other tried to run in the wind which was like running on the spot (picture some human leaning tower of Pisa) all the while I was imagining showing up at the emergency room & screaming

-It seems the rain has slit my face wide open
Will I need stitches?

& they would tell me there is no way to stitch up wounds inflicted from the heavens

-You would need a special kind of thread found only on the moon

Then I would die.

They would write me up like those people
struck dead by lightning or spontaneous combustions

My tombstone would read something like it rained on her
parade too soon or rain rain go away but really everyone knew
the r was a p and so it read pain pain go away & I still had not
settled on a proper epitaph by the time I had reached my front
door which during my absence had transformed into a mouth
that opened to swallow me inside to swim in the smells of
cinnamon and the saliva squeals of my children & later that
evening, after tucking them in bed I plotted my exit

But why?

I can still hear you asking...
Can only summarize as follows:

once the moon has beckoned
once you have witnessed a miracle
of light exploding
before your eyes
once you have been sliced through to bone
by a drop of rain
life on earth
simply
will not do

Sue MacLeod

Brick Lane

Sometimes the coming together is so sweet
we'd gladly break apart for it.
We fought our way through Hackney
from Stoke Newington to Brick Lane Market
each sway of the bus
that bumped your leg against mine
was a new affront,
tossing together
what ought to be asunder:

                                        you

          & me

                    "we're *through*
          when I get back to Canada."

     "Then go" you snapped.
The wheels rolled

                    over,

                         over.

               Far cry

from the day we sat up top
on another bus
& peered through the rain-streaked windows,
you riding look-out to one side
& me to the other, for a splash of purple
in a grocer's bin — lovers
wanting only for the sky to close
& ingredients
for eggplant parmigiana.

Not eggplant but *aubergine*
here in your country. I rested
my hand on your knee
& savoured things foreign
but in my own language.

       Water

wasn't pooling in the gutters
    this time
but at the rims of my eyes,
 me holding down
       the sight
    & sound of something breaking —
not a graceful giving-way like weeping
but unhappiness's answer
to a huge
guffaw.

     Below us
your city unfolded raw
as nerves
& by the time we reached Brick Lane
barbed wire
was strung on many
lower balconies

★

"not four not three oi'll tike"   there were trays of petunias   & you
saying, *why can't you just believe*   " 'av some lavly marigolds"
lampshades with tassels gone yellow   "oi'll tike TWO POUND FIFTY!"
" 'ere ya go, Squire"   the boots they were selling were   *why can't you*
just believe I love you?   full of holes   *why can't we stop this once &*
for all?   "izza vejdibble chopper, mite"   lava lamps   backscratchers
"cuts SHARPERNANA rizer!"   ashtrays like skull & crossbones
" 'ow kin ya pass it up?"   & then coming through the crowd

a shrunken " 'ere ya go" planet's whole stockpile of unwanted "ya
won't git a bedder price anyplice lidy, izz–AL stolen" a shrunken old
man with stubble & rheumy blue eyes cradling *why can't you just
believe* cradling *I love you* cradling a live white rabbit in his arms

★

What would I tell you
        if I knew you now?
How handsome you looked in that spring
of your fortieth year?
But those are easy words
when what I mean is elemental: you were
man to me.
I remember the salty
cracked voices of the hawkers
when I started to cry,
when I *began to weep* then,

        "whazzamadder luv?"   "y'awright dear?"

The old man's water-
colour eyes
& the pink eyes of the rabbit —
they seemed frozen
in a snaking line of people
and a squiggle of bare concrete
might have been
                a forest path
we were waiting turns
to take. I turned away
into the good-leather smell
of your jacket,
your arms coming round me,

    "What's he *doing* with the rabbit?"

my lips   brushed
the base of your throat
& you said

                    "What is it?
                         What is it about that
             that makes you so sad?"

How could you not
know? it was
        everything —
not so much that something could shatter
      our lives
but more the way we go on even after
something has.

We saw
through different windows,
all right...

★

I'd tell you
I've long forgotten the cause of that fight
but not the gentle pressure
of your arm around my shoulder
as we left Brick Lane, left
all the sad dresses & miracle
gadgets, caught a bus & rode it
like a thread pulled
on the bias,
the tapestry of London,
the trip home always shorter
than the one away

★

I'd tell you, sometimes
when my hand comes to rest
on the curve of my hip, where the body swivels,
I know that I still carry
how we'd take each other, steer
each other home. Back
in your bedroom, our clothes washed away
with an urgency like summer rain
we moved   together
hard enough   to wear the edges off.
Then, under cool sheets,
the heat of life coiled in our intertwined legs
& your breath on my neck

you drifted into your own view, looking
for whatever   splash
of purple,

      & I drifted back

        to Brick Lane...

    was he taking it home
      to *eat* it?

           was he taking it home
          for a pet?

       did he hold it   for comfort?

     had he *brought it*   to the market
   for the walk?
the sights? for air

I lifted your arm from my shoulder,
rolled into the gaps in your sleep-heavy breath
& dreamed he was living
in a room just above,
dreamed your street had grown meaner

to meet him, your walls held a chill
& the home-from-teaching clatter
of your housemate
in the hallway
faded to a
shuffle, drifted
into footsteps on the floor above,
a creaking of springs,
the man breathing,
the rabbit
too soft to pick up.

Susan Goyette

To Get Away

I've crossed roads, avenues, des boulevards,
des chemins, lanes, crescents, streets,
highways and freeways, the road to success,
the yellow brick road, memory lane, the long and
winding road. Even the chicken crossed the road to get away
from my house. And across the road

were two doberman pinschers, a seven-foot long
python that hung from the crabapple tree on nice days,
and the neighbourhood unemployed mechanic
who sold hash and did tattoos on the side. His backyard
was a car cemetery, dead-eye headlights and opened,
twisted hoods. In the corner, a cage of rabbits
for the python to swallow whole.
                                        It was heaven.

Next door to him was a man who lived alone who lived
next door to a man who lived with his wife. The two men
were in the middle of an electric hedge-trimmer war. The wife had nothing
to do with it. They took turns. While one of them trimmed
the hedge, the other would scream. They started trimming
early in the morning, sometimes late at night. The hedge used to be
up to their shoulders. And while their trimmers whirred, the wife

would skip across the road to the yoga instructor's house.
He grew marijuana on his back porch and hung boxer shorts
on his clothesline. The electric hedge-trimmers could only go so far
plugged in.
                And across the road

was a pen salesman and boxes of paper, a set of twins
and a woman who looked like her poodle. There was a house
haunted by a dead man in pyjamas. Across the road
were mirrors you could look into without having to
look away. The stairs went up and stairs
went down, the welcome mats worked. Snow
would melt first across the road and the nights
were shorter. And the rabbits, the rabbits

across the road wanted to be, even begged to be
swallowed whole.

Christmas Past

The dining room table is set
with china and silverware, the image of us
nested in serving spoons talking about
                    the weather.

Buffalo got snow. So did Toronto. My father is carving,
has carved, will carve the bird. He takes more pleasure
in this than he should. He has rows of baby
food jars downstairs filled with nails, he has a staple
gun. And clothes he wears that blend him into
                    the landscape.

And the dog chases, has chased, will chase the cat
until one smoky October night when he'll chase her
right into the street. The cat will watch the dog
from the opposite curb as a car, gunning around the bend,
hits him. The dog will lie, twisted, on the road
thinking: this time, this time you got lucky.

If it's snowing in Toronto, we're going to get it next. Snow
and mashed potatoes. Shovelled, shovel, will shovel.
Shovelling back gravy and stuffing, my sister makes happy,
hungry noises and my father stirs his tea; his spoon
and the china teacup, cat and dog. This whole family is cat

and dog, a blizzard and a bus, shovelling,
shovelling to get out of winter, to get out
of this snowbank of a dining room with its platter
of carved bird and the dog finally asleep under the table
not even thinking about cars, the cat cleaning, has cleaned
will clean her paws, wash her hands of us all.

Heather Pyrcz

Prelude on Prospect St

in memory of Tommy Troke

When all is said and done
what have we seen on Prospect Street?
Sunrise in the east and after a fiery day
the red sun setting in the western end
We've seen the lilacs laid low crushed
by the weight of march snow and ice till
twenty years of growth snapped or bent
so low the roots heaved up
We've seen the students come and go
like Fundy tides — quick and high and utterly
predictable: in they come as green
as grass and young as spring and out
they go sobered by the weight of growing
old, they hold behind their eyes
We've tracked the path of mars, counted
moons, and heard the mourning song
of shooting stars
We've seen pileated woodpeckers mating
in the maple tree, a racoon birthing,
skunks digging in the night yard;
one year a merlin devoured pigeons
who know all there is to know about
strutting but very little about hiding
We've picked wild flowers that grow on the
south bank where women, too drunk to walk,
have slept all night uncovered and unseen
wrapped in nightshade's poisoned dreams
Construction, deconstruction
and its appropriation
In the northern gloom we could become cynical
but then light breaks and every year
love is renewed on Prospect Street
we see this, too

No matter what happened the year before
— break up & disaster — worlds falling apart —
walls crumbling — lives shattered — it doesn't matter
love is a word on Prospect Street that spreads
like warm butter or burning oil on water
like spring grass or tulips pushing through the ice
under the lilacs

What have I known on Prospect Street? A friend
til yesterday when the black hearse pulled up to
Tommy's curb. A grey march day. Drizzling rain.
And in that moment, all I'll ever know of birth
and death and how the one engenders all the rest
And love. All I'll ever know of love. How love
is all there is between the poles

for Harry Thurston

groundless,
the sandpipers are flocking on the dyke
an aerial performance, a dazzle
of light and dark in sudden shifts
of illumination; great cascades
of curves, sea spray, sea wave,
an elastic banner of illusion
Where is the beginning and the end
where the centre? dark mass
wing to wing, they rise and fall
as one thought: *inseparable*
hold the ever shifting centre
and turn their bright side to the wind

Lynn Davies

Briefly, Abelard Tries To Understand

Abelard, the cat, who's been
around, would have his friend, Manon, believe
that life is God inhaling, and that death
comes when God's nostrils are empty. She says, Abelard,
why do you keep hunting with the neighbourhood cats?
They fight over leftovers and brag of feasts.
Who do you know besides bully raccoons, a few skunks,
and rats? He murmurs, life could be short
if God becomes asthmatic. Besides,
what else is there to do?
    She cleans an umber-coloured paw, and says,
one day I swam out to the islands
at the harbour's mouth where seals watch land
that never floats away. The water so foreign,
and willing to feed me to the red-eyed fish
circling below. Court a bird, make it your friend.
Or carry a mouse still warm to the coyote
who claims the unlit alley behind the restaurant.
See if he thanks you. She lies down under ferns
curling from the ground, and he remembers the time
she insisted he listen to the red poppies
pull their petals in at dusk. All he'd heard was the ocean
grieving for something he didn't understand, eyed the crow
in the tree for the contents of its shiny belly.

Tonight the Violent Wind
(Christmas Eve, 1992)

In the rockingchair, by our tree wearing lights,
carved birds, red sleighs, I listen to John
pound the last minute details into a gift
for our daughter. Our children sleep at last,
while a choir on the radio sings
for the one born in a barn so long ago.
    But yesterday, under trees not far from here,
a trapper found the weather-raked bones of a human being,
all that's left of a teenage girl
who disappeared here last New Year's Day.
                  The papers report
autopsy in progress, foul play suspected.
Residents of the area wonder why she lay
undiscovered for so long, hidden in the grass,
only a stone's throw from the grove of birch trees
where people walk their dogs, stop and have a smoke
all the time. So bleak, the way the road ends
for the young woman leaving home with a backpack
like me, some twenty years ago.
                    Downstairs
he completes his gift: the workbench, fitted
with a vise, 2 clamps, a handsaw and hammer.
    Tonight the violent wind is a gift,
the way it rips scarlet bows from the house
across the street, enters our home to give me
the smell of old ashes in the bucket by the stove.

Shari Andrews

Imagining the Catacombs

These tunnels take on the same dimensions,
the same lack of light as my chest cavity.
Ribs of stone close in on my lungs.

Except for this difficulty breathing
that I bring on myself,
it should be easy to follow those who guide
down into the bowels.
After all, no soldiers pace above ground
ready to point the cold tip of a spear
between my shoulder blades,
a sword at my throat.

And those torches can't lift themselves
from their brackets on the dripping wall
to scrutinize my darkly pumping heart.

The Smallest Rafts She Can Imagine

She goes down to the banks of the river,
wades to her waist.
Her skirt, a lily, blooms on the surface.
Her legs, the plunged branches of a birch tree.
In her belly, a clenched fist.

She had intended to tear her words,
leave not even a single one whole,
but now she sees it is better
to put each page face down in the water,
let them float, perfectly flat,
the smallest rafts she can imagine
lying on, drifting away.

Words becoming smudged ink,
hieroglyphics that fish nibble.

She turns, moves back toward shore.
Slips and twists on stones,
flaps her ostrich arms,
sheds water.
Her skirt, petals close
around her newborn legs.

Anne Simpson

A Head Like Hers

Shave my head,
she told her son. Hair was falling
out in clumps anyway,
and she had no use for it. He didn't
want to do it; think of the care
needed to raze that scalp

egg-smooth. Her husband
came to help and the two of them
worked slowly. She could see
their reflections in the dark
window, felt the little blades
of despair. What if none of this

did any good and she was
pared down
a little at a time? The moon was rising
above the garden and slightly lopsided: a head
like hers. Anthing can invade

luminous places. The moon
had marks to show for it.

Now What?

Everyone rushes in
past the lawn where someone — fenced in —
kneels to check the sprinklers. We keep close
as bees, past the paddlewheel boat
and Tom Sawyer's island
all the way to Splash Mountain
which is closed, temporarily. A woman circles
with a baby in a polka dot stroller. Now what?
Everyone is at a loss. Even Cinderella's castle
is under repair (the moat lacks water
and men are fixing it). Things glazed with heat
waver, diminishing in size. And Snow White,
with her paste-coloured skin, cherry lips,
is perspiring. Here's the mouse
with a helper who says that anyone wanting autographs
will have to line up. I watch, under the jacarandas
in the heavy, perfumed air,
rubbing a little dirt between my fingers
to see if it's real.

At night we ride the bus back — swaying
from side to side — to our hotel, wearily
picking our way through towels by the pool
shaped like a guitar, where children are jumping,
wreathed in sparkles of water. Up they go
and down, every little jewel.
In the shadows of the rose garden,
just past the pool,
A skinny girl in a white bathing suit
tells her boyfriend — her voice high,
harsh — that she came here to have fun.

On the last morning, we see the huge tree —
made entirely by hand — at the centre
of another theme park, the newest and best.
Stilt walkers plumed in yellow and blue
stalk around us like spoonbills.
It's the hottest day yet. All we can think of is water
and shade, but there is none. A child flings
a video camera on the ground. "Stupid bugger,"
shrieks a woman, and then a man scoops up the boy,
gives him a bottle of juice. The peacock imitates
the sound. I hold my children's
hands so tightly they ask to be released.
They ask for water, which I don't have.

There are tears in my eyes because of this
or the plight of lions
splayed on artificially heated rocks,
giraffes staggering through landscaped forests,
heads moving this way and that
with the slightly lunatic and bewildered look
of things captured
on America's funniest home videos. And it's late, it's late —
perhaps we'll miss the quaint little train
that takes us to the African village
where we run all the way to the exit,
smiling and nodding
at the driver who asks how we liked it
as we sink down on the plastic seats of the bus.
It's over. We have postcards, maps, souvenirs:
everything to help us remember it
the way we're supposed to.

J. Maureen Hull

Brain

The brain is a maze of corridors, crumpled grey passageways, innumerable secret rooms, trapdoors, underground tunnels, close and private forests. Facts, faces, landscapes drop in through your eyes, ears, nose, skin, dreams, are lodged inside and never again retrieved. Countries you don't remember visiting are mapped and coded in your brain. Latent skills rust or fade in lightless attics. It is impossible to know all you know.

Blood rivers away from the main stem, branches into small tributaries, smaller streams. In the backwoods where capillaries thin and thread, in distant murky backwaters are people you've never met   they are your barefoot kin, the ones with underground lives who know survival lore. They know you, and they have watched you bury things. Though you make yourself forget at once, they know what you have abandoned, they know location, time, and event. You fishtail the surface of your life, flatter yourself that you understand motivation, sequence, result. You are more than you know.

Heading North

Everyone here is heading north,
their denim coats with sheepskin linings
laid on plastic chairs.
Technicians guard their heavy cases,
(equipment, papers, booze)
fearful that some reckless teen
might liberate a tripod
and take it for a joyride.
Everyone smokes — even the kids.
Flattened clouds of white and grey
canopy sleeping infants.
Children blitz the candy machines,
and the guys in the corner
top their cans of Coke with rye.
Scientists pace and fret and pace,
review their projects, over and over,
desperate to pry as many samples,
facts, and figures as they can
from the short and brilliant summer.
I'm traveling light: clothes,
toothbrush, a brand new journal
stuffed in a seasoned knapsack.
Traveling light, all eyes and opinions.

"Yes, it's pretty," they say,
pleased with my enthusiasm.
The sun's gone down,
come right back up,
skipped off the earth
like a stone in slow motion.
We're drinking single malt scotch
that arrives by the case from Inuvik
on a once-a week Twin Otter.
Tw'otter, they're teaching me to say,
these guys who won't admit to
their first heart-stopping reaction
to the landscape, the light,

the blue-green mosaic
periodically carpeted
by a thousand acres of fireweed.
They talk, instead, of garbage, oil spills,
permafrost integrity,
chopper time, and research grants.
This gives them a moral edge
on ignorant tourists and feckless poets.

Racketing thunder overhead,
a blade that bites the sky and pulls
the great glass bubble aloft.
Icebergs drift beneath my feet;
there are whales, they tell me,
in that blue.
We're spilling oil on Herschel Island
to track where it goes on the tundra,
and someone's collecting arctic flowers,
stars that twinkle underfoot.
Everything's being so nicely explained —
such a waste. None of it's going in,
not nomenclature, reproductive data,
or numbers of litres per square meter.
Nothing that isn't colour, shape, smell.

Apples from the Hudson's Bay
are two bucks apiece; I make pie
with the skins on. At that price
I'm tempted to include the cores.
We polish up the crumbs
as we listen to the evening news
at the end of a dial and a finicky wire.
Names and places from a time
when we lived in cities
under a smaller sky.
Earlier, as I lay on deck
soaking up the August heat, daydreaming:
whitefish, wolverine, caribou,
something white and elemental
sifted from the sky.

September: we huddle over a kerosene stove,
parkas zipped to our chins.
Sleet scores the portholes,
furrows on the stern
and when the weather breaks, we bolt.
The pilot stands on a pontoon
rocking the Cessna back and forth
to break the surface tension.
The mirror ripples, shatters,
lets us go reluctantly
as if it knows we won't be back.

Regina Coupar

legacy

the soil of
Nova Scotia
is red
red
as blood

it holds the
bodies of my sisters
who cry to me
from their graves

I hear their voices
in the wind
I see them dancing
in the forest

they are my
roots
I am their branches

together
we make our offering
to our daughters

Sophia rising

sophia rises
slowly

she makes
her
way through debris
collected
during a lifetime
of random hoarding

she climbs
through the tangle
of borrowed
images and ideas
which clutter
the heart
and strangle
the mind

she pulls away
the filth
and rot
which stick to her skin

she stops
to pick a
darkened bouquet

from the mire
and carries
it with her

as she breaks
through the
surface she
holds out her
wilted bouquet

I receive her
offering
and begin to
feel her power
as she continues
to rise

I raise my eyes
to the sun
give thanks
and
continue
the journey
with her

Deirdre Dwyer

Promises

She is walking to work, thinking
about the view from the kitchen window:
blue clouds above the horizon
like sad balloons,
a plastic bag caught in the tree
that a month ago was a flood
of yellow leaves, the tree holding on
to that bag as if it were the last leaf,
as if it held promise,
what the wind keeps tugging at.
She is looking at rivers of ice and snow
on the sidewalk. Hours later they will have shrunk
to pools, undefined shapes.
She's thinking about the wind that churns
the snow in the air. Some flakes will never make it
to the ground, will be distracted
by wind. Could you be satisfied
with a life like that?

Perhaps the snow is distracted
by something else, she thinks, something
we haven't noticed yet, may never understand.
Small animals hear frequencies
of sound we can never eavesdrop upon.

When cars drive by, she asks,
what do they make of this woman?

She is thinking, for some reason
that may have to do with her stride and the wind,
the pull of muscles in her thighs,
of how she will feel, later that night,
when she climbs on top of her husband,
when she will absorb his hard cock.
She thinks of flakes of snow churning
up and up and up. Some of them might land
on the cloud of their birth.

The Last Swim

As if the water's coolness wants to gel
or crystallize, it shimmers
turning your underwater body
a careful, precarious mosaic, a pottery
glazed with a crackle finish,
the veins and splinters of a shiver.

The water holds you temporarily
like a teacup we hold to the light,
imagining where it will break
when it's dropped.
      You shudder
thinking of that deed performed
intentionally, with some kind of malice.

The last swim of the summer is a dying
love affair, where hope is palpable,
where, after the love-making,
you try to contain
the pleasure.

E. Alex Pierce

The Snakes Transform in the Woodpile

Even the eyes moult, growing larger
under the skin that covers them, a skin
that thin, purely transparent, holding them
intact, so they can do their work. What do they see
at the moment of moulting — the snake
that was, the snake that will become — split,
blind, as the lost world that memorizes itself, still
present in the cells that lift off
as light as paper?

        Under the lids,
a questioning takes place: *inward,*
outward? —The netted retina
receives a dimming light. The final eye
looks inward, sighting back
along the spinal tube, the aperture
quiescent, until a rippling signal
prompts the inverse motion,
peeling then from now — and ends
the doubled world.

        Which must be
what her eyes see, as she lies, old woman
in her hospital bed, old aunt staring out ...

        Watching her sleep,
three nights now — the convulsive turning
weakening her — an arm got loose,
inscribed the air, it traced the hand
along her shoulder, round the hairline,
then her breast, all shrunken in, but curved
the way that hand was touching it.

Saint Pete's*

I am walking in water, like all the summers of my childhood. It is the green, the colours of green laid one against the other — the familiar dirt under my feet, crossing through fields belonging to someone else, a visitor, not a stranger, the sense of simple content — that take me back there from here. I am rendered twelve, without the ecstasy, but with all the sureness of belonging, hearing every wind's breath as a sound for me, the liquid air a fluid accompaniment; the noises of the swathing machine and the watering cart, the hammering on the roof, necessity not intrusion. Since I belong, everything belongs. In the still heat, I can hear the caragana pods splitting as they let go their seeds.

In the monks' perennial garden, each of the plants has a presence: they are monarchs, some already cut down, but still impressive, like the delphiniums — enormous plants with hundreds of leaves, and thick stalks that carry the complex blue flowers. Now the veronica is in bloom — spiky magenta and rose pink — and late lupines the colour of rose madder. The gladioli have been carefully staked, herringbone flower cases part to release the citron yellow blossoms. A single hollyhock bends, curved to the wind. They are each half-wild, half-tamed.

Something follows me, something benign. Or is it just that nothing follows me, nothing stays long, not even the happiness. There is a continuous breathing in and breathing out. An hour passes, then a bell — another hour. Each one marked and noticed, measured equally: here is three, then four, then five. The fullness passes to another fullness; relief to agony, agony to relief. What's done is done and no one hurries.

* *Saint Peter's Abbey, Humboldt, Saskatchewan, site of the Saskatchewan Writers' Guild Artists' Colony.*

Eleonore Schönmaier

The Names We Carry

     Syllables scuff
low branches.
      "Do you really know where
we're going?" Jen asks.
        "Hear the sea?" I say.

     On the stones
a seal's leather coat. Clustered,
cleaned: the vertebrae,
ribs, pelvic bone.

Jen collects sea parsley
for our salad.   "My son
died two years ago," she says.
Sonya bows
     to storm-petrel
       wings
on the seaweed. The dog races,
mouthing
     an unearthed bone.

The four men: do they
      notice
the coast strewn
     with abandoned
imagery?

The boughs
a neighbour marked
to trim for me
            still bend.
He hiked his stretch
of shore,
        slipped and plummeted. His name
is one
the men carry.

I scrape away bark.
Scarred trees border
a sheltered path
for we trespass
by a cabin, the table set
for the dead,
            but they dine only
in our absence.

What we don't think of packing

but take along anyway: the shoes on our feet,
the fifty-four bones in our hands, the memory of
the colour of the sheets on our beds. We prepare
for flight as if we and the customs officers are the only

ones who will ever open our baggage. Nightshirts close
to the suitcase's zipper so when we arrive we can quickly
begin to restore what we thought we'd lost. Certain kinds of loss
we bargain for in transit: eight hours of sleep,
the memory of where we parked the car —

In Canada a man stands at the end
of his driveway talking to a neighbour: *I received
the call — search and rescue. There was no screaming, no
arms hanging loose. The helicopter shone light on the water
and we picked up what there was —*

*When I walk the beach with the kids
I know what I'm looking for.
I found a piece of plane and slipped it into my pocket.
Didn't tell the kids — a scrap
the size of a two dollar coin.*

Loss jangling, except it's in a currency
no one else understands even if they were on the boat
when he cupped the child's sneaker in his palm, insisted
the police promise to return it to the family — We never

anticipate losing the memories of what we have already lost —

Margaret McLeod

No Wolves, I tell you

In the forestry display booth
at the Exhibition, I'm the woman
who holds the jaw bone of a deer
in the palms of her hands.
Standing beside a forest ranger,
I show you the differences
between a coyote pelt and a wolf's.

There are no wolves in New Brunswick,
I tell you. That's what the biologists tell me.
(They also say eastern coyotes claim
wolves for close cousins,
but I don't want you scared
when you put out the garbage tonight.)

At the forestry field day,
I'm the woman who sits
behind a long table covered
with the excrement of animals.
At the entrance to the wildlife trail,
I challenge you:
which animal made this heap of pellets?
I surprise you:
the twiggy blue mess was made
by the same black bear
who left the tidy brown pile.
The difference is blueberries.

The ranger who did this job last year hid
a pile of glossette raisins on the table,
asked you what they were,
popped one in his mouth.
Grinned at the expression on your face.

We tell you there are no wolves,
even if you think you've seen one.
You didn't, just a coyote,
devouring your cat,
piling deer bones
in your back field.

No need to worry, it's just a coyote
slinking through those trees,
plotting how to take my lunch away from me.
The big bad wolf would want more.
Coyote's just a poor relation,
won't bite too hard.
Relax.

Late at night on game patrol,
when there's nobody around
but owls and field mice,
some rangers believe in panthers.
Dark ghosts that cross the road
in front of a car, a camp,
scream in the woods behind you.

We none of us ever feel the danger
that passes within a few yards:
bear, lynx, coyote, poacher.
What's drawing a bead on your back,
or staring down at the top of your head.

Ghost child

i

a little girl is there beside the roadside in a thin white
nightgown   I haven't seen a house for miles   she's a flash by
the side of the road

I drive past   can't get her out of my mind   thin little white
arms   ghost   no cars   no houses for miles

so how could she be there

but I'm tired, scared   it's january 5 a.m.   icy   I'm pregnant
have to get home   I keep driving   refusing to think of who
she might be

ii

the child who belongs to the wild cannibal family   who hunt
on the road between newcastle and fredericton   they heard the
car coming   thrust the child out into the road to get me to stop
then they'll fall upon me   drag me into the woods to a shack
torture and rape me   eat me and my baby   crunch at our
bones

iii

the child who stands by the side of the road holding out her
arms to me   I stop of course
humanitarian   human   good person   she does not speak when
I gather her into my arms but she is very cold   I decide to take
her with me   to find the next house   to find a home to find a
telephone   I must save this child   I place her gently in the car
I'm afraid a killer will run out of the woods with an axe   a
paper bag over his head

I place her in the car   get in and drive away

I drive talking gently to her but even going slow it isn't possible
to look at her often

AND

*   she turns into a monster with huge green teeth and
  glittering eyes

*   she's holding a knife and her eyes glitter   she grins and
  whispers hoarsely in a man's voice   *pull over*   *pull over*
  I'm going to kill you

*   I turn towards her and she is gone   only her little white
  nightgown is heaped on the seat   I stop the car   check
  the back seat   but she's gone

iv

bone eater
eater of flesh
dragon
heavy scaly smooth flesh
cruncher of bones

bone eater
I reach out my hands
toward her and scream
as she devours them

v

I pass her by   leave her out there in the woods in the dark in
january because I believe all those other possibilities   they've
all happened to me over and over

I go home   crawl into bed and sleep holding my belly my
baby   I wake up   make myself some toast and hear on the
radio that there was a fire   the mother and father escaped but
the little six year old girl hasn't been found   police are asking
for anyone who may have information to call

vi

but I know this child was being abused by her father when she—

vii

no   it was her   the little girl   who set the place on fire
because mommy and daddy had been making her play that game
again and they'd locked her in the basement   she climbed out a
basement window and ran in her bare feet through the snow to
the road

forget the fire

mine was the only car she saw before her father roared out of the
woods and ate her

viii

or she set their house on fire because of the game   then ran out
the door and down the road to the highway   where I passed her
by

she wandered down the road   her parents burned to death in the
house behind her   finally she got sleepy laid down in the ditch
no one will ever find her

ix

how about if I stop   put my arms around the cold white child
hold her to my rich belly   pick her up and place her gently on
the seat of the car   I take off my warm coat and tuck it around
her then I push down the car lock and close the door   go
around get in my own seat and drive off   as I pull away a man
with an axe comes running into the road   he has a bag over his
head and he roars   we drive faster   faster   desperation giving
us courage to drive like this in spite of the ice

we get away   I drive the little girl home with me   we get
back to the house   lock the door behind us   I call the police
they never find the bad man   no   they do and he turns out to
be her father   he goes to prison   I adopt her and she becomes
my daughter and sister to my baby   she never speaks

or

she someday opens her mouth and her sounds are like angels
singing

either way   we live happily ever after

The Poets

Listening to the Voices: Carole Langille

"I remember talking to someone very wise. She said, 'If you ignore the voices, they'll keep coming back.' Every voice has something to tell you. If you say, 'Well, what is it you want to tell me?' then you can sort it out. Some of these voices are incorporated from our mothers, our fathers. If they're addressed, you can learn a lot. Maybe that's the difference between prose and poetry. Prose is: 'I want to say something; how do I say it? What's the most skilful way to say it?' A poem is 'What is this poem saying to me, and how do I release the message?' "

Carole Langille grew up in New York City. As a teenager, she wandered around Greenwich Village, hoping to be invited to artists' salons. Carole studied writing at Brooklyn College. She has worked with John Ashbery and Carolyn Forché: In the late eighties, she moved to Lunenburg, Nova Scotia. Carole is the author of a children's book, Where the Wind Sleeps *(Roseway, 1996) and two collections of poems:* All That Glitters in Water *(New Poets Series, Baltimore, 1990) and* In Cannon Cave *(Brick, 1997). Carole is also a visual and ceramic artist.*

Carole and I talked at her home in Lunenburg. Shortly after this, her book In Cannon Cave *was shortlisted for the Governor General's Award.*

Why did you choose poetry as your form?

Well, my father was a communist. (laughs) Everything was channeled into his political views. He thought poetry was not worthwhile unless it had to do with workers or making boots or selling bread. It was sort of a narrow view. I wrote as a very young kid. I remember reading Stephen Crane's odd, quirky poem to my father, and he said, "What is this nonsense?" So it was like trying to prove that poetry was important.

There is prose I love, which is thrilling. But most of the time, I don't want to spend hours and hours composing a sentence. I want to spend hours composing a line. That seems like valid work, so that each line is beautiful. I don't want to render a whole world. I want to get a moment.

How do you "get a moment?" Can you describe the process of writing?

Often, I'll write down a word, a thought, a sentence. This either comes from when I overhear people talking or when I'm talking with friends. My friend Alexandra said, "People forgive so much." I wrote that line down in a poem. I try to keep these scraps of paper together in a wonderful brew pot where I can just reach in and take something. Short lyrical poems sometimes just start with a word — "ratchet wheel" — and I think, "I can do something with this." I have an idea of what to write, and then the poem explains itself to me, and emerges. Then it takes a long, long time. I enjoy it, but you know, I think there's something manic about a poet. Borderline case ...

What is writing poetry, for you?

There are many reasons I write poetry. I'd like to think of it as spiritual practice, as something I do with the desire to enrich or enliven or ennoble. It is so easy to sound pretentious when talking about this. I feel great resonance with Octavio Paz when I read that, for him, poetry was "a means of access to pure time, an immersion in the original waters of existence." He said poetry is going "beyond ourselves to the encounter of ourselves." When I write, it is to tap into this inner world and to "bear witness" to its tie to the world we live in. And I guess what moves me the most is a certain honesty and courage.

You want all the senses to be awakened in the poem. Sight is very apparent to the poet. Sound is important, too. Much of the poem is what you hear, whether you're reading it on the page, or someone is reading it to you.

How has moving to Nova Scotia affected you?

When I lived in New York City, I would read Elizabeth Bishop's poems, and she would talk about *Nova Scotia*. I always thought, "What a nice word," and now I live here. (laughs) When I first came here, I went to where she lived.

I clearly had to get out of New York City. It wasn't a good place for me. And because I had such a connection to Nova Scotia years before I got here, I think that's significant. I feel like I'm home. I feel like I have a family here, too. I'd like to feel like I'm flexible enough to move, but it wouldn't be easy for me. It's been such a nurturing place, and I feel safe in my home. And how many places in the world can you walk where there's no one else there?

How did your work first receive exposure in Canada?

Dennis Lee was reading his book in Halifax, and he came out to Lunenburg. My friend said, "Dennis Lee is here!" and I said, "Who's Dennis Lee?" I hadn't been in the country that long. I sent him my book. He sent copies to different people. I owe a lot to Dennis Lee for introducing my work to people.

Who is your community of writers?

I used to be in a workshop with Sue Goyette, Sue MacLeod, and some other poets. It's important to me to share my work. It doesn't have to be a local community. I write letters, too.

You described John Ashbery earlier as "the poet of atmosphere and thought." That could describe your work equally well. Do you think the "atmosphere" and landscape of Nova Scotia have entered your writing?

They have. There's a lot of landscape in *In Cannon Cave.*

Where is Cannon Cave, and why is it important to you?

It's at The Ovens Park, a miraculous place in Riverport. It used to be a Mi'kmaw gathering place. It's a very powerful place. You walk into the Cannon Cave and you hear, boom, the cannon. There was an incident in my life where I actually was in the Cannon Cave. Something happened there. I came to Nova Scotia because I got married. My husband took me to Cannon Cave right away, and he said to the water, "This woman is going to be my wife — I want her to hear you." And the water started roiling and swirling. I know it sounds ridiculous, but the water responded to his words, revealed its awareness. At night, the water is phosphorescent.

You seem interested in hollow spaces, containers. A cave is like that, isn't it? In your poem, "Her Kind," there's a reference to a woman who makes vases out of hollowed-out rocks.

I know a woman who makes vases out of hollowed-out rocks. It's wonderful.

In the same poem, "Her Kind," you talk to Anne Sexton. Why did you decide to have a conversation with a dead poet?

The poet Liane Heller said to me, "Why did you choose to write about Anne Sexton? I think that's an important question that you have to address." I took this long walk on my very special beach; all I thought about was Anne Sexton, and she did answer me. It was a very powerful lesson — if you're open enough to what they have to say to you, there is a very strong spirit that comes through. Anne Sexton said, "Nothing will pull you under" — what a remarkable thing to hear. Especially because she was pulled under, you know. And Liane said, "Now you have to have a dialogue with her." This is one of my longer poems, which got me to wanting to risk more, to see how I can stay in the game longer, because often you want to pull out when it gets too hot. You know what I mean? (laughs)

I remember talking to someone very wise. She said, "If you ignore the voices, they'll keep coming back." Every voice has something to tell you. If you say, "Well, what is it you want to tell me?" then you can sort it out. Some of these voices are incorporated from our mothers, our fathers. They stay with us. If they're addressed, you can learn a lot. Maybe that's the difference between prose and poetry. Prose is: "I want to say something; how do I say it? What's the most skilful way to say it?" A poem is "What is this poem saying to me, and how do I release the message?"

Besides being attuned to environments, you seem very interested in lighting, too. In a poem in In Cannon Cave, *you look inside a tree and see light. Why is light important to you?*

There's a lot in my poems about lighting because sometimes I look at my world and it seems like it almost doesn't exist. These images of light and shadows come to me; I don't plan them. I wouldn't have even thought I use a lot of doors and windows, except people point that out to me.

What attracts you to houses?

I love houses. I draw houses. And once you draw a house, it becomes your house, which is really interesting. Mark Strand has this wonderful line about walking with his wife. They pass a house and he says, "ours all the more for not being ours." I think that's really true — something is so much more yours just because it isn't your responsibility, or your life. Abandoned houses have an impact on me; you pass an abandoned house and there's something very special going on.

In many of your poems, I sense struggle, the speaker's struggle to negotiate her way through the complex landscapes of life. Yet there is a centredness, too. A hard-fought-for affirmation of self. You've written, in In Cannon Cave, *"These days on walks I knock inside me and it's strong and hard as oak." How, in writing poetry, do you "knock inside yourself?"*

You know when you have that knock inside you, and you feel something that's not fear? But I think you have to know fear to know the great relief of feeling that it's not there.

Do you see yourself as a poet with, essentially, a redemptive, or affirmative vision?

I do feel extremely positive – Pollyanna, to the outrage of some of my friends (laughs) – very grateful and hopeful, at this time.

I recently had a powerful and important experience. My father died in June [1997]. I was able to see him before he died. I felt I was brought there by something greater than will or desire. My father stayed alive, I felt, to see me, to see all his daughters in the room. He was very loving, very kind. There hadn't always been that good feeling between us. I feel this is sort of proof that I am taken care of, that the forces will carry me to a positive place, if I go with them. I have more trust, since then. There does seem to be a lot of beneficent energy to help us.

John Steffler said in a book called *Poetry and Knowing* that all poems, no matter what their subject matter, are a desire to clarify, to make some order. It's true. The powerful thing is to listen to the voices.

M. Travis Lane and the Art of Layers

"I don't have a message. If I had a message, I'd put it into prose. Most of what I'm doing is feeling out a cadence, a sound, a feeling. One does, I think, interrogate one's own experience as a way of getting from the beginning of the poem to the end. I like to 'pack,' and have as many layers as I can."

M. Travis Lane came to Canada in 1960. Educated at Vassar and Cornell, she wrote her Ph.D. thesis on the poetry of Robert Frost. For a number of years, Travis Lane reviewed poetry for The Fiddlehead. *She is an Honorary Research Associate at the University of New Brunswick. Her work was first anthologized in* Five Poets: Cornell, 1960, *and her first book,* An Inch or so of Garden *appeared in 1969 (New Brunswick Chapbooks). Since then, she has published numerous books of poetry, including:* Poems 1968-1972 *(Fiddlehead Poetry Books, 1973);* Homecomings *(Fiddlehead Poetry Books, 1977);* Divinations and Shorter Poems *(Fiddlehead Poetry Books, 1980);* Reckonings: Poems 1979-1983 *(Goose Lane Editions, 1987);* Solid Things: Poems New and Selected *(Cormorant, 1993);* Temporary Shelter *(Goose Lane Editions, 1993);* Night Physics *(Brick, 1994). She is currently at work on a collection of poems entitled* Solar Remission.

Travis and I talked at her home in Fredericton.

What were your initial impressions of the Maritimes?

When I first came here, there were two things I noticed. I think this is changing. One is that people in class, particularly girls, did not speak up as readily as the girls in Cornell or Vassar. They were much more shy. Even when I taught a graduate class, they were so shy. We hadn't been here too many years when we went to a reading of poems by young people. A young girl read her poem, and it struck me as really quite good. Afterwards, I came up to her and said, "That was a fine poem, and you will be much less nervous next time." And her friend, who was with her, said, "Of course she is nervous, she is a woman!" The idea was that women don't read poetry in public. I related this to the Maritimes; the Maritimes are a little bit late in terms of women's assertiveness. But Alden Nowlan, too — for him and his background, it was very eccentric to write poetry. The idea of writing poetry was not a problem for me, but I can see that it has been a problem for quite a lot of Maritimers, particularly for women Maritimers.

The Maritimes are interestingly different from New England, but they're not that different. Many people have family who have gone to Boston. Bangor is closer than Toronto or Montreal.

What sense of literary community do you have? Is your community here, or elsewhere?

Most of my communities are not communities around writing. They are people who respond to beauty — beauty of behaviour, beauty of action, making beautiful things. So some of the people with whom I feel community are artists, musicians, gardeners, lovers of nature, or activists for peace and the environment.

As a writer, I'd say my primary sense of community is through books, in particular, the nineteenth- and twentieth-century poets. I read earliest and most in American literature, so I feel a sense of community with Walt Whitman through Robert Lowell, and of course, Emily Dickinson, Elizabeth Bishop, Marianne Moore. Everything one reads becomes part of the community, in a sense, because you respond to it. And there's a sense of the community of *all* poets.

I do know some people who write together, but I don't see the sense of that. I've never been in a workshop. I do, however, attend readings by local poets whenever they're held in a smoke-free place. We have a lot of good writers and I hope more serious scholarly attention will be paid to us than has been done so far.

Did you have particular mentors in the early phases of your career?

No mentor at all, just everything I read.

Can you talk about the importance of regional venues for writers, and regional presses?

I think they are extremely important. This is something we should always have. People have to start, and if you have an inexpensive thing you can give to people … all these little readings … it's just marvellous. It gives you a feeling that the community is alive. I'm so glad Joe Blades is doing this now because back when

Fred [Cogswell] was doing these things, there weren't as many public readings. But he was keeping things in print. And Nancy Bauer was doing chapbooks for about two or three years. This was at the same time as Fred Cogswell's publications. It keeps the region alive. It gets people started. *Pottersfield Portfolio* is starting to do some things, too, in the region.

How do you think being a writer might be different for a woman?

I can think of two differences. In one case, I think it's changing; in the other case, it has not. When I was in graduate school, there was some feeling that women did not have the experience. Women were rarely in the trenches; no woman could say that a whale ship was her college. What could women say? All they could do was, like Jane Austen, write on their little inch of ivory. There was very much that feeling. People are beginning to realize that women are getting more experience, that a lot of men didn't have much experience either, and that there is plenty of excitement on the home front, too. Making fun of a woman for being over-ambitious for her "small" experience — I think that's gone. But that was certainly present when I started. But the other thing that has not changed — you go to any conference or reading or large group of poets, and a male poet is thought of as glamorous. He is surrounded by male poets who admire him and lots of young women who admire him because he's a poet. For a woman poet? There are no young men admiring this important, sexy old lady.

So a woman poet has a strange status in our culture?

Oh, she's a witch. Definitely. Women aren't supposed to do this, still, somehow.

You've written long poems as well as lyrics. What determines the form a poem will take, for you?

For me, a poem begins with, basically, a cadence of words. And this will already decide whether it's going to be short or long. Sometimes I have done a group of short poems that seem to be related. I just did a group on bad weather that won a prize in *The Amethyst Review.* Other times, I know that I want to do something with a very sizeable subject, but I've also got the cadence and idea. For example, in *Divinations,* the one that won the Pat Lowther award, I wanted to do a sort of divine comedy. But I had to work out a plot, and then feel my way into those. Those three are the longest of the long poems. *Night Physics* starts with a series of meditations. In the last one [in *Night Physics*], I got interested in the Harlequin figure, and in patterns of three.

Your "Local Suite" captures both the spirit of the long poem and the shorter meditational lyrics within it. You described that poem as an "experiment in minimalist writing." Can you talk about what that means?

There has been a lot of very minimalist writing in Canada. Some of it, I've found, takes almost too much sympathy from the reader. I tend to like to "pack," and have as many layers as I can. I like to write "thicker," and ever more thicker. But I thought it would be interesting to write as thinly as I could, and still enjoy my own work. That is the "thinnest" poem I've ever written.

The last poem in "Local Suite" contains a violent attack; where did that come from?

That actually happened. This town [Fredericton] has this idea of itself as a nice, pastoral place. I like the idea of the whole "Local Suite" getting spookier and spookier. It was terrifying; some ordinary person was walking downtown and someone took a hammer and hit her on the head. No particular reason. The "Suite" began with everything nice and charming ...

So are you trying to subvert a regional stereotype of pastoralism?

This may be Arcadia, but death is there, too.

Can you talk about regionalism, with respect to your writing? A number of your poems, like "A Stone from Fundy," depict nature in terms of its regional particularity.

One should try to *live* where one lives. If transplanted, put out roots. I've travelled all my life and I have my literary background. But coming here, and making friends and learning of the community ... I wrote a poem about Memorial Day in Fredericton which begins "Most happy of all cities, Fredericton." "Happy" because Fredericton thinks of wars and other dreadful things as always happening somewhere else. Cradle of poetry, Loyalism, the pastoral self-image. I am reminding people of Fredericton's image of itself with a sort of affectionate irony. It's interesting to use the past voices of a place, as well as its present voices.

So immersing oneself in place is connected to time, as well as space?

You're never out of time. History shapes so much of things. I'm culturally allied. One can't help absorbing some of the voices and attitudes of the region in which one lives. In some senses, I'm culturally alien in the Maritimes, but I'm also culturally joined.

Can you give me an example of what you mean?

A story — I hadn't been here long, and I went downtown and bought my little daughter a Canadian-made dress. I took her to Sunday School, and the people there said, "Oh, what a beautiful dress! You must have bought that in Boston." When I first came here, there was this tremendous excitement about England, and about Boston. And while they were extremely fond of Fredericton, there was this odd sense .... Another story is that my daughter, who grew up here, went to the University of Toronto. And she was kidded about being from the "backwoods." Fredericton really isn't the backwoods. It's got books, it's got radio, it's got TV. Some years later, I heard someone giving a talk, and the speaker said, "Canadian poetry began in the Maritimes, then it moved to Montreal, then it moved to Toronto, and now it's out West!" (laughs) One of the things one learns about a region are its sore places, all those little edges. To some extent, Maritimers have felt and have been treated as colonials.

Also, some people feel there's something old-fashioned about liking nature, or the woods. They think you sound a little too much like a nineteenth-century writer. And everyone knows that Maritime poets write a lot about nature, when contemporary poets write about other things. Certainly Maritimers as a whole are very aware of and interested in the natural environment.

I'm thinking of your poem, "Ah! Wilderness" — the point of view is that of the landscape that is being violated by industrialization. Does your writing have an environmentalist dimension?

Very much so. There are quite a number of my poems which refer to or comment upon contemporary physics as well as biology. I think a poet should be aware of contemporary ideas and problems. And "nature" still has to be thought about. How should we live in the world? I'm not against industrialization, but I do write out of love for natural beauty. I hate ecological disasters, pollution, greed, waste, stupidity, destruction, ugliness. We have to fight for beauty, wilderness, natural diversity. We have to write out of love.

W.H. New describes your poems as being "interrogative," asking questions. How is writing a way of questioning?

In a sense, for me, that is the shape of it most of the time. Because I don't have a message. If I had a message, I'd put it in prose. Most of what I'm doing is feeling out a cadence, a sound, a feeling — the experience of meditation. One does, I think, interrogate one's own experiences as a way of getting from the beginning of the poem to the end of it.

New remarked, too, that observation and composition seem very closely bound together in your work. What do you think he meant by that?

New was probably drawing attention to what might be called in my writing the theory of the organic: that language and perception should not/cannot be separated. A theory or opinion can interfere with our seeing an alternative beauty or an alternative idea.

Is that what you meant when you've written about your "resistance to theory?" Are you saying that theorizing does a disservice to poetry?

I don't think a theory does any disservice. But to be rigid in one's approach ... An idea will come into fashion, and we will start seeing it that way. Like all women are hysterics ... we no longer think that, but we did have that idea. The kind of theorizing I dislike most is when you decide that everything is plus or minus, black or white. Dog is not opposite of cat. The world just doesn't come out that simple.

Your poem about the cat — "The Long Way Through to the Chairs" — suggests that, and in doing so, issues a challenge to dogma. (laughs)

The grand truth is not necessarily the shortest distance between two points. What the cat says is that the experience is what matters — to the cat. The mind should allow itself to explore beyond the rigidities of map, language-set, prejudgement, or myth.

Mary Dalton and the Process of Poetry

"The idioms in Newfoundland are still very rich. My work is pre-occupying itself more and more with those idioms and rhythms, the energies of Newfoundland speech. There is nowhere better for a poet to be, with her ears open, than here."

photo: Rod Batten

Mary Dalton spent the first sixteen years of her life in Lake View, a small community in the parish of Harbour Main at the head of Conception Bay. She received an honours degree in English from the University of Toronto. Her postgraduate study took place at Memorial University of Newfoundland and the University of Liverpool. She has published two books of poetry: The Time of Icicles *(Breakwater, 1989; rpt. 1991) and* Allowing the Light *(Breakwater, 1993). Mary Dalton won the 1997 Government of Newfoundland and Labrador Arts and Letters Poetry Award as well as the 1998 TickleAce Cabot Award for her poem from a series entitled "The Tall World of Their Torn Stories." She teaches creative writing and other poetry courses at Memorial University of Newfoundland. Through her creative writing course at Memorial she has fostered the craft of poetry within the community. Four collections have been published as an outgrowth of that course:* Currents, Sundogs, Twig, *and* Wild on the Crest: Sea Poems: Newfoundland and Labrador. *An essay, "To Capture the Sound of Water: A Language Denied," on the influence of Newfoundland speech on her poetry, is forthcoming in* The League of Canadian Poets Living Archives Series *in 1999.*

Mary and I talked in St. John's.

Who were your earliest literary mentors?

When a friend asked me what the dedication of *The Time of Icicles* would be, I jokingly replied that it would read "Despite all you bastards." But it wasn't like that at all. In childhood my reading and writing were encouraged by my mother. She loved books and snatched what time she could from her days of steady work to read. She had taught me to read and write before I began school. Both my parents possessed the gifts of language and music that I believe have nourished my own abilities. And in high school at Harbour Main I was lucky to encounter a teacher who relished literature and who fostered our impulses to write. She was called Sister Jude Thaddeus then; she was a Presentation nun. She was Anne McCann from Western Bay, I learned later. She influenced many of us, I believe. The novelist Patrick Kavanagh was one of her students at the time as well.

But after that I was set on my own path. I had no mentors because I didn't look for any. I wrote not because anyone encouraged me but because the words wanted to come out of me. When I did show my poems to Patrick O'Flaherty, he urged me to publish them; he gave me courage, the ability to separate the writing from the self, to put it out in the world. His good word meant a great deal — and it still does.

Who have been important mentors and/or literary contacts since, and at present?

What's most important now for me, I think, is the sense of being part of the tribe of writers, of conversation with other writers about matters peripheral to the art of poetry, as well as about books we've read, readings we've enjoyed. Membership in the League of Canadian Poets and participation in the work of the League has helped to strengthen that sense of belonging to a community of poets, as has my contact over the years with various Irish poets through my work in Irish Studies. There's always been a keen sense of connection with the writers and other artists of Newfoundland.

When and where did you first publish your poetry?

During the first half of the eighties I was co-editing and co-publishing *TickleAce*, a Newfoundland literary journal which began under the auspices of MUN Extension Services in 1977. During that period I returned to writing poetry; I had been writing in my late teens but had turned away from poetry to literary criticism for many years. It never occurred to me to send the poems out in the early eighties. I was writing in solitude — no workshops, no discussion groups, no editing by friends. The poems were somehow invisible to me. I was preoccupied with editing, reviewing, analysing others' literary creations, teaching. What prompted me to think more about this dimension of my writing — it sounds ridiculous but there it is — was the sight one day of the stack of poems on my desk, the sheer height of it. I decided to post a bundle off to Patrick O'Flaherty. I knew Patrick only slightly then — he was a colleague, but I knew him mainly through his writing as an astute (and a stern) judge of literature. Eventually he came to my office one afternoon with my bundle and said in his brisk way, "You're a poet, you're a poet — you should get a book out." (laughs) It was like being confirmed by the bishop. Patrick recommended that I submit a manuscript to Breakwater Books. I did so — with the result that I actually had the manuscript accepted and a contract for the book before I ever saw a poem printed in a literary magazine. Only much later did I realize how unusual that was.

What things do you think distinguish Newfoundland women poets from women poets in the other Atlantic provinces and elsewhere?

I don't know that I can speak for other Atlantic poets ... what I have observed, however, about the poems of Carmelita McGrath and Agnes Walsh and about my own writing is that, while we are quite different from one another in technical matters and while we each have our own voice, we each have a common preoccupation with the landscape of Newfoundland and with its history. Perhaps there is also some sense of embattlement within the Canadian context. And Carmelita, Agnes and I have all grown up outside the city; our experience is rural, marine. Our background is Irish-Catholic. That has an effect on the rhythms of the writing; many of the rhythms of Irish Newfoundland speech are close to the rhythms of Irish English.

The women poets of the Maritimes may themselves be affected by similar forces and grappling with similar issues. I can speak only of Newfoundland — and perhaps warily even of Newfoundland. I am leery of generalizations of this sort. But I will venture to say that in Newfoundland there is a grounded quality in the writing; it is grounded in a culture and in a landscape, seascape. It seems to me that the preoccupations of other Atlantic women poets are not so much those I've just mentioned.

What does link the women poets of Newfoundland with their sisters in the Maritimes is the exploration of matters of identity as women; that links us with many women poets elsewhere as well. Always, however, matters of history and politics and language as they are traditionally conceived of are intertwined with questions of gender for us here in Newfoundland.

Not all, but some of your poems are satirical. Can you talk about where the satirical thrust in your work comes from?

Satire always has a contemporary edge to it. Some of the poems in *Allowing the Light* and *The Time of Icicles* examine the relation between Newfoundland and the rest of the country. I'm not sure that the satire is emerging from being colonized for a long time. Newfoundland had a period of being its own country. It lost its government; then it ended up being passed over from the British to Canada. Does the tendency to satire come from living in a colonized country? If you write in a colonized country, you might be thought to lack confidence. You might be thought to have a sense of inferiority. But you could think of it another way. If you're thinking of writing from a space that has a long and complex and rich history, and that has its identity defined geographically, as an island ... well, maybe we're writing out of confidence, writing our satire out of an impatience with what we see sometimes as the arrogance of the rest of this Canadian entity, the condescension towards Newfoundland. However, some of the satire, of course, directs itself at matters of class and social oppression and gender.

Poems like "Larry's Nightmare" in The Time of Icicles *contain satire similar to what you're describing — a resistance to the "imperial centre" of Toronto ...*

Yes. That whole question of the relation of the centre to the periphery — the periphery is only the periphery as defined by the centre. Once you look at the "margin" and see how it defines itself, it may be another thing. It's a central question when you're thinking about cultural politics, but not when you're thinking about the art of poetry, and the development of your own body of work over time. When you're talking about the arrogance of the centre, you're talking about the media, and the whole apparatus of the discussion of a culture. But you're not talking about individual poets, often. When one meets poets from all over the country, they're working on their craft, and one has more in common with them than not. These questions about centre and margins have been formulated as the central questions about our literature, but sometimes they strangle or they stymie discussion. If you're talking about power, some poets from certain areas might think they don't have the same kind of access to the means of discussion. That is true; what do you do about it? You either move to the "centre," or you do your work where you are, and you do what you can. It was very freeing for me to realize that Toronto is a region. I often find discussions emanating from Toronto on CBC Radio quite parochial; there's a good deal of complacence. Smugness is not good for art. It's probably more freeing to be on the outside. The questions about cultural politics don't engage me as much as they did.

If this matter preoccupies you less now, as you say, what things preoccupy you?

I'm thinking about how to make a first line, about whether my poems are developing in terms of craft. I'm thinking about the poetry of Anne Szumigalski and Don McKay and Dennis Lee, just at the moment. For me, the really exciting thing is to talk about poems, whether they're mine or somebody else's.

How do you situate yourself as a Newfoundland writer?

There's a map, a print, called "The Newfoundland-centred Universe." It's a map of the world drawn by a contemporary artist so that Newfoundland is at the centre. The map calls attention to the conventional map as only one version of reality. I live in a Newfoundland-centred universe; we are at the centre. I am becoming more and more comfortable with that notion. I don't see that as narrow at all, since my mind ranges over the globe; my reading is not by any means confined to the literature of my own culture. But in finding what Seamus Heaney calls the "energies of generation" in my own language, I'm embarking on what is for me the necessary poetic task. It has something to do with reclaiming vital aspects of self.

I have been spending more time outside St. John's, in the bay that I spent my childhood in. What I have found there belies the glib generalizations about the passing of this and the passing of that. We're assured time after time that we've just become part of this global culture. But the language of the people here is extraordinarily resistant to the homogenizing effect ... they all have televisions, but they don't speak like the television. The idioms in Newfoundland are still very rich. My work is preoccupying itself more and more with those idioms and rhythms, the energies of Newfoundland speech.

But to some extent, I think that interest in the vernacular is reflected in your earlier work, in poems like "taxi dispatcher jazz." Your recent work reflects an almost total immersion in the spoken word, in Newfoundland idioms.

Yes. Although these poems are rather more like collages than photographs.

Your earlier work was more rooted in a literary, written tradition and in mythology, wasn't it?

Yes. But the odd mythological allusion still crops up. A recent satirical poem called "Oldfella and Mr. Subaru" takes on the business of the Newfie joke. There has been no radical shift in my writing; the preoccupations were always there, but isn't that true of most writers? If there has been an evolution, I hope that the work is becoming rhythmically stronger, that there's a deepening, a strengthening, of the craft.

Many of your poems seem, in some way, to examine process. Do you want to comment on that?

Your observation that my work has always examined process is right on the mark. That is what unifies all my poems: the fleeting, kinetic energies of the voice; the fleeting energies of the earth. They're unstable, always in a process of change. What's going on in a garden is in a process of change. Language itself is sounded, moving. I have a fascination with the kinetic. Does that preoccupation distinguish me from other poets? I don't know. I doubt it.

Are your botanical poems, your poems about plants, gardens, a way of examining process, too? I'm thinking of a poem like "Winter Garden," for instance. "[S]ay partridgeberry" is another example of a process poem, a self-reflexive text in which the speaker looks at her own process of inscribing the words on the page.

I do tend to have my literary-critical discussions in poems. That one is really saying, "Look to your own language." The amaryllis, I suppose, could stand for the whole body of work that is literary. The partridgeberry is a blazing, rich colour like the amaryllis, but it has these little berries that cling to the ground here, in Newfoundland. What you said about process is very interesting; that's what most of the poems seem to be doing, looking at process. If you look at the content, the voices speaking, the garden poems, the language poems, I think they're all manifestations of a similar impulse.

Your new poems which use the vernacular are often quite minimalist, brief, like dramatic moments. Why?

They're little bursts of energy. There's this brief speech, this out-rush of energy. Each one is small, but contains, I hope, pictures of whole worlds. A whole world emerges in that voice that rushes by you. There's also that sense of danger in the landscape, the weather, but that cheery energy in the face of it, you know?

Where do you come up with descriptions like "He had the face of a robber's horse?"

These are other voices speaking through me; these are idioms.

"The face of a robber's horse" is an expression in Newfoundland English, as is "He'd drink the rum off a dead Nelson." They used to preserve the bodies at sea. Nelson was preserved in rum, so the saying refers to someone with such a thirst, so greedy, that he would drink the rum off a corpse. These are the gifts of the language to me. Why would I feel inferior, or have any sense that I didn't matter quite enough because I was in Newfoundland, as opposed to elsewhere in Canada, when the language gives me these gifts? There is nowhere better for a poet to be, with her ears open, than here.

To a reader outside Newfoundland, most of these idioms can be understood through context. But what is "sparry"?

(Laughs) That's the one word I made up. It does not exist. It's coming off the verb "to spar," as in verbal play. Several people have asked me about that, so I say, "Hey, this is my contribution to Newfoundland English." My very own invention, said the White Knight.

You're from Conception Bay. Are some of the idioms in your work particular to that area, or would they be known throughout Newfoundland? How particularized is the language?

Many of these words and expressions I have heard; some I have not. The map of our language is *The Dictionary of Newfoundland English.* Some of the words I have simply come across in print. But what happens is the whole association in memory, so the rhythms you're hearing will be of Conception Bay, and even more specifically, what we call the head of the bay, these Irish-Catholic communities. You can't even speak of Newfoundland language as a monolithic entity. There are areas of Newfoundland where the language owes a debt to Shakespearean English. A word might start something else going in my mind, but the rhythms of it, the cadences, are going to be from that area. It's those voices. What the poems become is a picture of language from all over the island, but the rhythms are of my area, because those are the rhythms I know best.

Are there any characteristics of these rhythms or idioms?

Much of the speech is of the body — the hand, the eye. The idioms are concrete, sensual.

So are there words in your newer poems that people from outside Conception Bay might not be familiar with?

Some of the words ... there might be very few people in the community who would still know them, especially younger people. In fact, one person reading these said, "You know, you are writing about ghosts." I disagreed with him because I have talked with people who use many of these expressions. But he said this because many of these words are not in common currency now.

Is this level of particularity a form of resistance to globalization, to homogenizing forces?

For me, it's observing the vigour of the speech, the concreteness of the idiom. For a writer, the language is your source. Of course, language is a very important medium of a culture. But I don't think of it as a resistance. Resistance implies that you're so conscious of what's there in the global culture that you're pushing against it, whereas I'm so conscious of what's there in the Newfoundland language that I'm celebrating rather than resisting.

So if you're celebrating language, you're not sharing the sense that some women poets have, of working in a "contaminated" language – contaminated because it is the language of the patriarchy?

I don't understand the concept of language as a trap or an enemy. Language has always been play, pleasure. Everyone owns language. I can think of when I was quite small, listening to people telling a story, or singing a song, or making a joke. I felt this playfulness, this pleasure, from an early age. Language was my realm, a place where I thought I had power. I don't see the patriarchal embodied in the very essence of language. If there are words you don't like, play with them, do something with them. Of course there are sexist and patriarchal assumptions in culture, but to argue that the essence of language is somehow polluted, that's a very different proposition.

Environmentalist concerns seem important in some of your poems. I'm thinking of poems like "plastic." In it, the woman wearing the Birkenstocks is trying to do all the right things, have all the right causes, but she still can't connect to nature in any authentic way. There seems to be a pretty pointed irony to this.

There's an irony, certainly. That woman is a way of mediating between the city and institutions like ACOA and the beach. The Birkenstocks and the woolly sweater are meant to evoke someone who is part of the ecological movement. She goes to the beach thinking she is escaping the plastic world, but the beach itself is polluted. This condition is all-pervasive. The dolphins dying of cancerous livers are dying because of the chemicals pouring from plastic factories into the St. Lawrence River. If you mean by environmentalism, an expression of the physical world as threatened, yes, that is there in "plastic."

Are you critical of how Newfoundland has been commodified and fal-
sified through stereotypes? Your poem "Lies for the Tourists" seems to
suggest this dynamic.

I'm glad you mentioned that poem in connection with our
discussion of satire. My satire is often directed at matters outside
Newfoundland, but I do not glorify Newfoundland society. Our
society is very rich, but it has got its own problems and contradic-
tions. That poem suggests we're complicit in the stereotyping we
experience. We create these "lies for the tourists," to some de-
gree, and to some degree, the tourists encourage us to lie.

Is a similar complicity suggested in "St. John's Day 1987?"

Exactly. Kevin Major's novel, *Gaffer*, is written out of horror
at Cabotry, the Cabot celebration. That is like "St. John's Day 1987"
writ large, a whole year of putting ourselves on display, of turning
our art into entertainment and tourist commodity. Ireland has done
it; many countries in the Caribbean do it. Our venerable leaders
seem to see it as one way forward.

Your poems use irony and satire sometimes to undercut the idea of
progress in the twentieth century. But you also use humour to reveal these
contradictions and problems. Can you talk about your use of humour?

If you observe the contradictions, you've become detached.
You have to, perhaps, be a bit on the outside, to see them. Why
do I use humour? Perhaps it's genetic. (laughs) I still can hear, many,
many years after their deaths, my parents laughing.

Liliane Welch's Fidelities

"All good writing is a praising of where we stand, wherever that is. It might be here, it might be in Europe, it might be the mountains. It's always the earth we are on. Writing is opening it up, so that others can participate in the event. Every piece of writing is a hand extended to a reader."

photo: Cyril Welch

Liliane Welch was born in Luxembourg in 1937. She received a B.A. and M.A. from the University of Montana. She holds a Ph.D. in French literature from Pennsylvania State University. Liliane Welch settled in Canada in 1967. She has taught at Mount Allison University for over thirty years. She has published fifteen collections of poems, including Brush and Trunks *(Fiddlehead Poetry Books, 1981);* Fire to the Looms Below *(Ragweed, 1990); and* Life in Another Language *(Cormorant, 1992);* Dream Museum *(Sono Nis Press, 1995).* Life in Another Language *won the Bressani Prize. Her most recent collection is* Fidelities *(Borealis, 1997). She has also published* Seismographs: Selected Essays and Reviews *(Ragweed, 1988) and* Frescoes: Travel Pieces *(Borealis, 1998). She has co-authored, with her husband Cyril Welch, two books of literary criticism. Among her many accomplishments, Liliane Welch is also an avid mountain climber.*

I talked with Liliane in her home in Sackville, New Brunswick.

When did you start writing poetry?

I did not start writing poetry until 1975. Before that, I was a literary critic. I started writing poetry in Europe, and never even thought I was going to publish it at all. I put it away. Then I got a phone call from a friend of mine in Sackville who said, "Nancy Bauer is coming to town [Sackville] for a workshop." So I went. Afterwards, I showed her some of my poems, and she said "I'm sure Fred Cogswell would be interested in these poems." At that time, he was running *The Fiddlehead* poetry series. I sent my manuscript in the last mail before a mail strike. I thought I would never hear about it again. Then we were eating dinner one night, and this woman came charging in with a letter from Fred Cogswell saying he would take the book. That was my beginning in poetry. (laughs)

Obviously, then, regional presses have played an important part in your career...

They are, I think, very important, not just for me, but for poets in general. I've been lucky; I've had books published in Ontario, out west. But the other books were published mostly in the Atlantic: Ragweed, *The Fiddlehead*, and Goose Lane. I think regional presses have a greater feel for their own region, but if they just confine themselves to their own region, they become incestuous and their view is haunted by extra agendas. So I do not believe that they can be exclusively regional; they have to let the fresh wind from the outside come in. Fred Cogswell was not a regional publisher, in that sense. He also published writers like Dorothy Livesay. He did not confine himself to this region. *The Fiddlehead* journal doesn't, either. We don't just have regional presses here; there are regional presses in Toronto, you know?

What is your relationship to place, as a writer?

I don't think I'm a regional writer. I love this place and wouldn't want to be any other place, but I travel a lot. The themes of my work are not confined to this place. There's an attachment to place that is not in this very narrow sense of regionalism. My books, like *Brush and Trunks*, try to capture the historical dimension of this region: the British lumberman, the contemporary hunter, the Acadian dyke-builder. Not every writer can fit into the "regional" category.

Who is your community of writers in Atlantic Canada?

I think we are very different here in Sackville from, for example, Fredericton. In Fredericton, people do have a writers' community. Nancy Bauer, for many years, used to run the Ice House there, where writers congregated once a week. We don't have that in Sackville. These comradeships, like you had in Boston with Lowell — we don't have that here. I personally don't depend on others; I've always been a loner. But then I live with another writer. What I have found sustaining in this region, and in Canada, is that people still write letters. I have a lot of ties with writers via letter. That means a lot to me.

When you first went to Montana, and you read a lot of American writers like Melville and Whitman and Faulkner, how did those writers affect your imagination?

At that time, I wanted to make my life in America, away from the old traditional societies. What I found in those writers was a voice that incited me towards freedom, into a different perception of reality. But at that time, I was not a writer. This was a literature that I imbibed, and still today, it holds for me this spirit of the New World that was so different from the Old World where I came from. So it was catching the spirit of newness, at that time. In Whitman, you have that "hitting the road," that departure, going into the land, letting yourself be embraced by it. I remember the open skies of Montana very much, and Whitman speaks to that — in contrast to the rainy and closed skies of Europe. In Baudelaire, you often have all this rain, the sky as a cover coming down, and everything transformed into a prison. None of that here. My husband and I take an hour walk every night down by the Bay of Fundy, and it just lifts my heart. I wrote the poem "Maritime Skies" in a moment of elation, confronting our open skies.

You have described your writing as celebrating the Maritime locale. How is writing celebratory?

All good writing is a praising of where we stand, wherever that is. It might be here, it might be in Europe, it might be the mountains. It's always the earth we are on. Writing is opening it up, so that others can participate in the event. I think that landscape, or place, is dead unless it becomes an event. Every piece of writing is a hand extended to a reader. I always smile a bit when I hear people talk about all the manuscripts they have in drawers; they say they want to keep them private. They don't want to give them to the public. That's not really writing, for all writing has to be going out in search of that reader who can participate in the event created with words.

So manuscripts in drawers will never become part of a community of words, or achieve what Don McKay has called "the small/matter-of-fact miracle of ears?"

Exactly. They are nothing. A book only becomes alive, an event, when someone does something with it. Then the community is being built.

Your writing often reflects on the act of writing itself. For example, you've written a poem about your pen. Why do you think your work has this self-reflexive impulse?

It may have to do with where I come from. The first writer I got very deeply involved with was Baudelaire. He was also a critic who wrote about art, music, and you have there the reflexive element. Mallarmé also wrote criticism, Valéry, Proust. I think it is good for a writer to reflect on the way the poem is made, because then you can put yourself into the position of the reader. If you never bother thinking about how this is coming out, what the intent is, then you can't imagine how a reader can respond to it. When I write my poetry, I don't think about theoretical questions. I'm an artist, working with the material. My life has been spent with a man whose profession it is to think about life, and about what the writing process is like. That probably influences my disposition towards writing. We walk about fifteen kilometres a day, and at night we do a one-hour walk, and when we walk, we talk. And that, I think, has something to do with the reflexive part, too.

Your book, Fidelities, *contains a poem called "Fidelity" about a painting by Alex Colville. Can you talk about why the notion of "fidelity" is important to you?*

What I meant was being loyal to three things: landscape, other artists, and home. I was very struck when I saw that [Colville] painting: the gestures of the man, the way the animal stands there, completely taking up the space. The man is only there because of the animal, because of his function of tending the animal. I think that painting is a symbol of Colville's life; he is a man who is completely there for his art. He is the servant of art. He would never let himself get distracted from his art. There's an extraordinary fidelity in the way Alex Colville lives his life.

Your own fidelity to art is strong; so is your fidelity to mountain climbing. You have written quite a bit on mountain climbing, but perhaps you would like to comment here on how mountain climbing becomes, as you put it in your poem "Accomplice" [in Fidelities] *"a postscript to writing?"*

The heights and the efforts that test are similar to writing. When you write, you're tested by the craft, the words themselves. When I go into the mountains now, we don't do technical climbing any more, climbing up sheer walls with ropes. We still do the kind of hiking other people call mountain climbing — very high, long, strenuous days. As I do all of that now, I can see that the two go so much together, that I got into one because of the other and it's kind of circular. My interest in mountains now is very different. I have become very interested in painters and sculptors. Giacometti, for example. When I go into the mountains now, they have an extra dimension for me because those artists responded to whatever it is that attracted me. However, these artists were not mountain climbers the way I was, at one time. But I cannot go through the mountains any more without remembering the paintings of these artists, and that gives my experience of the mountains a resonance that it never had before. When I was young, I was such a fierce mountain climber, that I thought, "When I can't do technical mountain climbing, hanging off these rocks, any more, I'll die, my inspiration will be gone." Quite the contrary — with art, these other dimensions have opened up to me, and the mountain, in some sense is much richer, even though I'm not hanging off the ropes.

When we first went into the mountains, I was awed by the sacred, the complete "other" I found there. It was just like going to church, but not an institutional church. Then we got into the technical, acrobatic climbing, and hanging there, you can't have any thoughts about the sacred or anything. It's just your cunning, and whatever you have to do to get up there. And when you get to the top, you're so exhausted, there isn't much room for any poetic thoughts, either. That part of our mountain climbing — the sacred — was completely gone. But now, with the ropes safely stashed away in my brother's attic — we can go back there again, and there's that initial facing of the "other" with all its poetic and sacred dimensions. And then, these artists ... I know mountain climbers who go into depressions when they can't climb any more, but they haven't been exposed to these artists. So in that sense, too, there's this fidelity to art.

Mountain climbing, for me, was very important because of the discipline. You have to be very careful, have to have a cleanliness in your life. I find that is very similar to writing — the attentiveness to the terrain, to what you are facing.

Your writing explores different personae, looks at things from different vantage points. Why does this interest you?

What is so magical about writing is that you can live the lives of many other people. Many of the things I write about have nothing to do with me, in the sense that I've cast myself as a character. In poetry, I would like to think I'm moving in the region of Proust who says that there are two selves, the empirical self and the creative self. The creative self is being alone in your study with your pen, the words; you are a changed person. When I was writing

Brush and Trunks, I had to play three roles: a hunter, a British lumberman, and an Acadian dyke-builder. All those are things that I've never really done myself. I interviewed hunters here in Sackville in order to get the techniques correct. I lost twenty pounds writing that. It took everything I had to get myself into these other personae. My husband saw me during the writing, and he said, "I don't recognize you." I think the creative self can be, literally and figuratively, quite somebody else.

In the poem "Together," in Fidelities, *you write, "I finally know/ how to descend." How do you get back down a mountain?*

The largest number of accidents happen on the way down. Usually, there is what they call "the normal route." Technically, it's easier to go down that way. So why is it, on that easier route down that should be child's play, so many people die? First, when they get to the top, they are completely exhausted. Also, there is an elation, so people get careless; they go down the other side in a more inattentive way. They talk and they let themselves be distracted. The descent is also an art. I mean this also for life. It is an art to climb down from the mountain from the highest peak of your life — to keep the spirit alive. There is an art to living well, a full life, after you're sixty. That's the descent from the mountain.

Medicine, Magic, Weaponry, Love:
Maxine Tynes' Poetry

"To write is powerful medicine, magic, weaponry and love. To write poetry is the ultimate in that power. I'm an East Coast poet, after all. The winds, the tides. When I sit down to write, all those natural elements are working on me just as surely as the available pool of words and phrases available to me are working on me."

Maxine Tynes grew up in Dartmouth, Nova Scotia, as did five or so generations of her paternal family before her. Her first book of poetry, Borrowed Beauty *(Pottersfield, 1987) was awarded the Milton Acorn People's Poet of Canada award. Maxine's subsequent books include* Woman Talking Woman (*Pottersfield, 1990*), The Door of My Heart *(Pottersfield, 1993), and* Save the World For Me *(Pottersfield, 1991), a children's book. Maxine teaches at Auburn Drive High School in Dartmouth.*

I talked with Maxine in Dartmouth's Alderney Gate Library. We met in the Maxine Tynes Room, which is about fifty metres from the old Tynes homestead near the railway beside Halifax Harbour. The room contains a portrait of Maxine painted by Rosemary McDonald. The painting's rich colours and depth do justice to the original.

Borrowed Beauty, *your first book, opens with a poetic contemplation of mirrors. This image of reflection, self-reflection, suggests that identity is an important theme in your work.*

That's very true. That essay on mirrors came from a sense of seeking self, and never quite reaching that definitive answer that one is looking for — whether you're looking into a mirror, or your heart and soul, or your intellect. At the time it was important to me to share that search. Those feelings haven't gone away.

In "Mirrors," you refer to having found a centre — but is identity a process, too?

Yes, a really healthy process. I find as I relate to a new facet of my life as a woman, as a person, as a writer, there are edges to be honed and new realities, and old ones, to come to terms with. It's very much like looking into a mirror, that depth perception, the questions: Am I writing from a true sense of who I am? Am I speaking with that voice that's true? When is it appropriate for that voice to be a collective voice, and when is it just mine, from my experience?

I've always admired the broad scope of your work. Your poems are sometimes public, addressing events that impact on a large number of people — like the Montreal massacre. But some are quieter lyrics, more in-ward-looking. In The Door of My Heart, *you seem to be moving, to some extent, into more private, inner space. Would you say that is true?*

The Door of My Heart is aptly named, I feel, for a number of reasons. It does represent opening doors to a more introspective interior, perhaps opening doors to aspects of my life which I have kept somewhat protected and have only touched on obliquely when it served the voice in the poem. It's not appropriate, of course, in every instance, but when and where it works, I feel that sense of reality first, and it's motivating to continue to explore that. It re-minds me of when I was a very young writer; I had a sense of opening my heart and revealing it all. But looking further along the time continuum, I really wasn't doing a whole lot of that.

Who do you have to trust to be ready to do that? What is it that allows you to go into the interior landscapes? Is it a matter of trusting your own voice?

I'm sure that's a big part of it. The other thing is the experi-ence of having gained acceptance for one's creative attempts. Even if everything hasn't been accepted wholeheartedly, there's enough of a positive response so that with experience, you feel, "Oh, why not?" But it's mainly learning to trust myself and finally getting to the point where it's more important to get that voice out, to am-plify that voice than to refine it to somebody's else's expectations.

Let's return to the theme of identity. Woman Talking Woman *ad-dresses this theme and seems to expand it to a communal sense, often, tapping into the collectivity. I'm thinking of poems like "Black Song Nova Scotia." How does writing poetry allow you to explore identity both in the sense of your unique self but also in the sense of the larger collectivity?*

I think poetry is a perfect conduit for doing both. The writing of poetry is very much like exercising all the activities associated with being a visual artist. If I were doing a watercolour, I would be preparing my brushes and pigments and all of that and at the same time, I would be looking out at the exterior landscape as well as trying to be attuned to the voices within. As a visual artist, I would be capturing the actual geographical plane or the group scene, or whatever. As a poet, I find myself dipping into a pallette and replicating a landscape of experiences both external, and private and intimate. I feel so connected to my own life and everything in front of me, I wouldn't really be able to change my impulse to capture both. That is as much of who I am as a poet as being introspective and sharing hidden fears or hopes or dreams or those kind of womanist realities that speak to me at midnight. Indeed, when I began writing poetry, long before I published, it was a response to being out there in the mix of what was happening, like taking the pulse of a crowd scene and translating that to poetic experience.

Can you talk about your earliest literary culture? Did you write as a child?

Almost non-stop, actually. My childhood years were fraught with the stimulus of being the middle child in a big family, and the older kids shared all kinds of reading with the little kids. We'd hear them doing homework and then at night, they'd have the responsibility of tucking us in. We'd get to hear our favourite stories, either from memory or from books. That inspired me to create and recreate those experiences for myself. Then as an adolescent, it became a big part of my personal sense of identity, to write my work. As a child, I wrote stories. In my teens, most of that fell away and I began writing poetry. Everything became a poem.

Besides the literary community of your own family, who was a mentor for you?

Almost from the earliest days of my public school childhood, as you probably remember, if there's anything about you that's noticeable, somebody who teaches you will usually focus on that and build that up to a point of recognition or usefulness, or whatever. For me, it was being a kid who wrote copiously — I had found some kind of voice that worked — you know, on a child's level. I always got really fine strokes for that. I can remember being walked around from classroom to classroom with some teacher holding an essay. Later, I found that other kids really didn't appreciate it that much. (laughs) At the high school level, that became

a really good thing. When I got to high school, my writing repu-
tation walked through the door before I did, so I was able to do
things and find a niche to fall into, unlike many teenagers who
wonder where they fit in. I was writing for the yearbook and the
school newspaper and getting involved in literary activities. It served
me well, and became something I could do and get pats on the
back for. My family appreciated what I was doing and let me know
over and over again. It must have given me a lot of personal satis-
faction because I kept doing it.

*So being a writer has been validating in a very profound way, for
you?*

Yes, I can agree with that without any hesitation. And in my
family, it was easy to get lost in a houseful of children. I always
had that role to go into, the reading and the writing, and that
gave me satisfaction. And my mother was such a teacher. If the
world had been different, she probably would have been a for-
mally trained teacher. She taught me to love words. Now, as a
teacher, I find I've turned into my mother. (laughs) My father prob-
ably did not complete elementary school. But he was the one who
made sure that newspapers came into the house. We would get all
the issues of *Macleans, Time, Chatelaine*. My dad could read, but
he couldn't write well. He could sign his name. He would have us
talk about what was in headlines, and you had to have an opinion!
If you didn't, he'd want to know why.

Being a writer gives one privilege, and gives one access to express
what we all need to and cannot always express. It's such a privi-
lege to be able to say to oneself, "I am a writer," because I have a
sense that women do feel connected, to a degree; yet for me to
careen down Spring Garden Road or at Portage and Main or on
Dundas Street, and to be emoting this, no matter how true it is,
people would look at me askance. (laughs) Yet as a writer, I have
the privilege of thinking as fully as I want to, and then spreading
that across the page in whatever it is that I'm writing. Then some-
body, that stranger who would look at me askance if I were emot-
ing this on the street corner, would pick up that page and find
those intonations of women who mean something to me and who
have influenced me. They may go off and do writing of their own.

What authors, stories, or poems impressed you?

Older sisters used to read classic stories to us. If there was a
childhood classic that I loved, it was probably *Alice in Wonderland*.
I was raised Catholic, and along with Nancy Drew mysteries, I

would scour the library for writing with a quasi-religious theme. I don't mean I was reading theology, but things like *The Robe*. It was turned into one of those *Ben Hur*-type movies with men in flowing robes carrying biblical tablets and looking down on the citizenry and pointing the big finger of morality. (laughs)

What about women poets?

P.K. Page, Atwood. In this region, Rita Joe — so many truisms all over her work. In terms of women writers of the Maritimes, anyone who is looking to find some realities and heart and soul in regional literature, I would steer them in Rita Joe's direction for sure.

In The Door of My Heart *particularly, there's a sense of connection with Aboriginal culture. How has that been important to you?*

It has been part of the context of my own reality, inside and outside of my world as a writer. Growing up here in the Maritime African-Canadian community, at a very early age I was somewhat aware of the influences on the development of my culture — not anything I had been exposed to in the formal education process, but certainly through my life experience. For example, we're sitting right here beside Halifax harbour. We're sitting right beside the railway. We're not aware of that because there's this beautiful steel and glass structure we're sitting in [Alderney Gate Library], but right outside is the railway. And my house was right beside the railway, maybe five hundred meters to the north of where we are. At that time, there was a viable, working railway system here. It served the regional agricultural community, the outlying rural communities. The passenger trains stopped right outside my back door. People would get off, and among them, Aboriginal women carrying their huge armloads of baskets to sell at the market. My mom would welcome them in. They would sit and talk over tea. I can remember our tiny kitchen being flooded with the baskets, but it wasn't just the baskets themselves; it was the room being flooded with colour, circles and circles of baskets. There was such a casual connection between my mom and these women. It never occurred to me that this was something to be writ large on my life; that these were women of another culture was not the primary thing. This connection between this isolated family and these women who were rather transitory at the time made quite a bit of sense when I thought about the early developmental years of this province: so many groups would not have survived to develop their particular cultural communities — whether we're talking about the Scots or the Acadians or the Black Loyalists. We all owe our survival and development to the Aboriginal influence. Here there was much less of the hostility *vis à vis* newcomers and Aboriginals than we found in other parts of Canada. Now there is documentation and recognition of support for disaffected minority settlers throughout Canada's coastal regions. There is documentation that my people, Black Loyalists, for example, and other African groups who settled in the Maritimes, owe a great deal of their survival and survivability to the reception they received and the schooling in the land: you know, how to cure yourself with the land, the vegetation. So in my heart, there's a kind of affinity. In my own family genealogy — it's very hard to trace in African-Canadian circles, unlike America, where various manifests were kept for economic and trade reasons; we did not deserve that luxury. On my maternal side, I'm convinced that there is a genetic link, some of my mother's people having settled in parts of Nova Scotia where there is a heavy Aboriginal influence. Just various traits that have survived, subtly, but they are true markers of the culture. This gives me a reason to embrace the cross-cultural connection that I know exists, certainly, on a sociological level, between Aboriginals and African-Canadians in this region, and particularly in my own family circle.

The baskets of the Aboriginal women you described connect nicely with Edith Clayton's baskets in your poetry, don't they?

Yes. Getting to know Edith Clayton was such a treat for me. She was a true matriarch of the Black community here. When I met her, she seemed to complete a circle for me. She was like a missing aunt, a missing grandparent. She was very warm, very engaging. She immediately recognized me as someone who was very welcome in her heart and in her presence. She often encouraged me to learn what she knew.

There are many other women in your poems, too: Portia White, Zora Neale Hurston, Alice Walker, Rita MacNeil, your own mother. Why has it been important to you to reach out and connect with all these women?

Well, we're a community. That's a given. As we move through our lives, we connect with women in our community. Then there are those other women who enter your life obliquely, who instruct you and who have no clue that for you, they are a light on the horizon, edifying your life. There are those women who give voice to what you have not yet learned; there might be women you would like to emulate or are emulating subconsciously. Maybe you have not yet found the strength or the life reality to voice that yourself. I'm thinking of women writers and artists and community leaders. As a writer, for me to intone the name of Edith Clayton, to describe Rita Joe — I'm thinking of the focus of her words and the strength of her ambition as a woman of her home/community/place and how she magnifies that to translate into something that has reality for me, a woman outside her culture but certainly part of the womanist culture, which is hers. For me, it's a given; it feels very natural, as surely as the texture of colour, light, sensuality, and women's politics is part of the fabric of my writing. It feels just as natural to embroider, to weave, to inscribe the very names, the lives, of those women, in my writing. It's something I do consciously, of course, but it's something that is working on me subconsciously at the time of my writing — as those other times I am moving about my life and I am infused with the power and the reality and the vision and the accomplishment of these women in my life, in the lives of women everywhere.

There's a lot of naming, in your poems. Why is that important? Is it a way of inscribing a community? A way of commemorating?

Yes. It is that. It's a way of creating the touchstone of community and accomplishment and reality, both historical and sociological. Feminist, surely. It's a way of creating a map, a grid, if you will — a poem that touches the lives of women could have been written in the most provisional of ways in which you develop and expand on the particular experience. Quite often, I have to people poems with the lives surrounding that experience, or the lives that form the foundation of that experience. Intoning the names, inscribing the names, makes them a permanent fixture of that experience. Perhaps there's something of the frustrated social historian in me. I often find that writers can wear that cap as well, and so often, the drift of women who have been a force within a particular movement, time, place, event, reality remains recognized and validated. There is an effort, not only on my part, but the part of other women writers, to raise our flag, in a permanent sense. And if we have learned nothing in the drift of millennia, the one thing we have learned is to make an effort to preserve the efforts of those who inscribe, who paint, who contextualize, who write. That will survive. To capture the essence of time and place and persona has, for me, a sense of value.

Let's talk about the themes of African Nova Scotian literature. In his introduction to Fire on the Water *(Vol. 1), George Elliott Clarke re-*

marks that romantic and sexual love are "rarely treated" by Africadian writers. But your work seems to contradict this, and offers quite a candid treatment of both love and sexuality.

We must explode the myth of that quote, actually. That quote is very narrow and reflects a narrowness of observation, and perhaps is a self-reflection of the writer of the quote. Of course I deal with issues of romance, sexuality, love, the physical senses, the whole notion of both pleasure and pain and emotional discord and harmony. It's part of my sense of being as a woman in the world. It was part of my experience in that early transition from childhood to young adulthood. I'm a firm believer that if one is a poet, one's work is a true litmus test of one's life. It is quite impossible to effect a charade on paper which will continue. That quote would be a paper boat that would sink quite quickly in the development of my manuscript, were I to try to drown out the voices which recognize and amplify those experiences in my life which taught me to be an emotional being in the world, a sexual being, one who recognizes that sensuality is part of the panoply of life. Even if I were not a writer, a poet, I have a sense that I would be a woman who would recognize those things, revel in those things, live through those aspects of my life.

This thing about being motivated by the various poetic muses knows no boundaries. I would find myself in difficulty if I stopped listening to emotions. For a poet to touch the life that is herself, you touch it all, whatever it is. Whatever that range of being is, it all emerges in the poetry. It all comes out. There are times when it is appropriate to lock off those more sensually inclined voices, but there are times when they must be inscribed too, in the finality of the piece.

Let me speak about the quote from another perspective. It's been my experience, having spent some years teaching African American and African Canadian literature that the earliest literature mostly did not deal with issues of human sexuality unless it was part of becoming a victim because of one's sexuality. That earliest literature, whether from America or another part of the globe, usually dealt with issues of survival in a world filled with markers not one's own. The diaspora declared that survival was key. So early slave narratives dealt with knowing how to be that mute, invisible worker. The writing of Zora Neale Hurston might have been an exception. There were the writings just prior to mid-century which dealt with new-found liberties, people surviving in urban ghettoes in the north. If you think of the development of Black music in North America at the time, it was fraught with sexual overtones. I'd have to say that Mr. Clarke is a little confused about some issues. There is a replication going on in the emergence of African Canadian literature — a kind of replication which finds its parallel in North American Black literature in general.

How would you characterize African Canadian literature?

It is mostly a literature of how we got from there to here, barricades we have gotten over; the Canadian canon must now make room for this new voice. But critics of the voice have to be very careful of what they're looking for. A comment like Clarke's is an important one because it gives all of us an opportunity to speak to the issue and bring our experiences to the table. What Mr. Clarke is looking for is probably there, but subtly, at this point. And once the time line progresses, as it will, comparable to the American minority milieu, we will find authors in all genres who are able to broaden their vision, their view, their creative voice beyond the particular survival reality. As for my own writing, it has, from the beginning, been filled with what is both a political, practical reality of what I've seen when I've looked around, including sensuality, sexuality. That's a reflection of who I am, how I have emerged in my life. In my case, the public "-isms" about me and the personal things in the shadows both emerged.

Let me ask you about the more political dimension of your writing. Has writing ever been for you an act of resistance? A weapon, of sorts?

Oh yes, from the beginning. When I look back to my earliest work, the one voice that rings through consistently is the political voice. The earliest youth poems were protests against war and wanting to encourage peaceful co-existence between cultures. I was doing two things. One, reflecting on what was playing across the world, and two, trying to impose my sense of balance. In my earliest writing, there was that constant reflection on the world. My dad personalized the world for us. He contextualized our life. I grew up feeling that I was a citizen of the world. That was an amazing feat in a middle-class household. And to add another wonderful layer on that, my dad worked at the government shipyard almost his entire life. He knew everybody, people from across the world. We might be sitting at supper, and there might be a Portuguese sea captain at the table. Someone from France, Spain, Russia. We'd hear the languages of the world spoken, taste different food. Those were my earliest childhood experiences. These experiences created a context for my life. It would have been artificial for me to shut off these voices. It was natural for me to address the issues of the world in my earliest writings, and it has continued. I was born with the universal spoon in my mouth. (laughs)

Do you consider yourself a regional writer, too?

Canada is filled with regional writers. I could not be Sharon Butala. Her subconscious terms of reference, the themes with which she was infused when she grew and developed were different from those which we developed here as East Coast writers. The minds and creative mandates of Québec writers are differently contextualized than mine. West Coast writers? I feel more of an affinity with them; we're both coastal people. Joni Mitchell would write about sitting on the West Coast, some island, watching the waves break. She was speaking to me, too. I'm a Maritime woman, too. Yes, we are regional writers. There are regional realities. We've been breathing them in from the moment of our birth. We relate to the world as people who have been existing, co-existing and surviving in isolation. That's a good thing for a writer. There's a regional flair and essence to all our writing. And Newfoundland? You know, there's a mystique to everything about the Rock.

There's the isolation. There's the development of culture separate and apart. There's struggle to maintain ties with the past and connect as obliquely as one wishes to the present. It is a reality that we are a regional nation.

But "regionalism" has been seen as a debilitating factor for writers in Canada, too, hasn't it?

To recognize that goes a long way towards diffusing the negativity of that and to embrace what is rich and real about it. And what you can't erase, you work with. We have suffered, as writers, because of regionalism. You have to recognize that. All the big publishers are in the golden triangle, central Canada. We have not developed our cultural institutions here they way they have been developed in central Canada or on the West Coast. There are all kinds of reasons for that. The smallness of the writers' community limits us. We don't have the full range of opportunities to connect with writers' opportunities, retreats, and so on. You have to step outside the region for that. Economics will often tie a writer to home base, when the writer is ready to fly. But you make the choice. It's the old "going down the road" choice that faces us, as Maritimers.

How much agency does poetry have to work towards creating a just and inclusive society?

That certainly is part of my mandate as a writer. When I wrote the first manuscript, *Borrowed Beauty* — everything that the writer is emerges in the first manuscript.

"Emerges" in a confessional sense?

Confessional is not the word I would use. Self-disclosing is. When one publishes a first manuscript of poetry, it really is an opening up of everything which is the essence of the writer. What are those things which are the construct of my essence? The cultural side of who I am. The presentation of the book clearly stated who I am, the rather generic face on the cover, of African Canadian womanhood. All the poems in the first book speak to issues important to me, feminist issues, issues of the world which end up at our front door, issues of poverty and place and the environment and armament. Very loud, strident voicings of those four things. The second book, *Woman Talking Woman,* is much more true to my womanist self. It's all bound up, however, in the four premises which construct the first book. *Woman Talking Woman* surely is the voice of a woman who wants to amplify the feminist side of who she is in a context which can relate to any and all women.

Some of these poems seem to have been written around the time of the Montreal massacre, including the poem directly about that. What kind of time was that for women?

It was hard time, an emerging time, a melding of the global community of women. Women were shaping that global community. There seemed to be a universal recognition of the emergent voice of women. The book *Woman Talking Woman* addressed the women of the world.

For someone who wants to learn more about African Canadian writing, and African Nova Scotian writing, what would you tell them? There has been Black Nova Scotian writing since the seventeenth and eighteenth centuries. But Black Nova Scotian writing is sometimes described as an "emergent" literature. Can it be both?

It's both because you have to look at the early writing and discover the context in which the early writing emerged. Most of the early writing was theology, sociological, quasi-academic. Those were the accepted purviews for minority voices, minority involvement. There was not the privilege of accessing local theatre or going off to some literary soirée. But for those writing for a more conservative construct, there were opportunities. In mid-century, more academic writing emerged which amplified a necessary mandate that had to develop. The latter part of the century here runs parallel to mid-century America, the Black artistic renaissance. That renaissance happened for a reason. Those people were the young adults of the first generation of liberated Blacks from the south. They were migrants. There was opportunity for those of a creative bent. Economics is a factor in terms of who emerged when. To a degree, that is an error; creative process emerges anyway. There is documentation of literary art by those who were enslaved. But certainly not at the rate of those who emerged later, those newly emancipated people who could hold jobs and sometimes access education.

I first heard you read your work in 1988. What has stayed in my mind was the strong oral quality of your poetry — its musicality, reflected through refrains, cadence, the surge and ebb of your voice. How has the oral tradition and, simply, sound, been important to you?

The oral tradition has been part of the Black community here since the earliest days of Black life in this province. It would have been part of the practice of faith, keeping a community's history alive. And recently, David Woods and AnneMarie Woods have been instrumental in developing drama. There are the natural rhythms in life, too. We are in tune with rhythms in our environment even when we think we are not. Somehow it melds with the ebb and flow of our own bodily systems. When it doesn't, we react. I grew up consuming everything ever sung by Joni Mitchell. What inspires one artist certainly is going to have an influence on a whole range of artistic sensibility. It's no mystery that there is a rhythmic choral quality to my work as I read it because I feel the ebb and flow and the surge of that choral quality as I'm writing.

Claiming Culture, Claiming Voice:
Rita Joe of Eskasoni

"The greatest difficulties facing
Native women writers is that they
are shy and have low self-esteem.
I did at first but got braver as time
went on. The applause is what
boosted my spirit. My knees were
trembling but sang after speaking.
At first, I was hesitant to write about
spirituality. Now I am more open
about it."

*Rita Joe was born in Whycocomagh,
Cape Breton Island, in 1932. Rita
began writing in her thirties, partly as
"therapy." Her books of poetry include:*
Poems of Rita Joe *(Abanaki, 1978);* Song of Eskasoni: More Po-
ems of Rita Joe *(Ragweed, 1988);* Lnu and Indians We're Called
*(Ragweed, 1991). Her work has also been frequently anthologized. Rita
Joe has been the recipient of numerous honours and awards, including the
Order of Canada. Her efforts to educate others about Mi'kmaw cultural
traditions have taken her on extensive speaking engagements.*

Rita conversed with me by letter, fax and phone.

Did you write when you were a child?

As a child, I wrote only my homework. I wrote once when I
was seven years old. I just wrote the words I knew, put them in
four line order. I guess it came out like an unusual poem; the teacher,
Bart MacKinnon, asked where I got them. I pointed to my heart
and head. It was only one time. Today, I think something hap-
pened that day that decided my future. I never for a moment thought
that I would earn all the awards that I have so far. There is an
opera in production in Holland by Hank Alkema, using my poetic
words in music. We will hear about it later.

In your autobiography in The Mi'kmaq Anthology, *you mention*

Pauline Johnson. When did you first read her poetry? Were you aware of any Native poets, female or male, during your school years?

Only Pauline Johnson, during my early school years.

You have written that you really began to write in your thirties. What prompted you to begin? Was there a particular event that compelled you to start writing?

In my thirties, my children were in higher grades. They brought home some bad stuff they read in books. My husband was a counsellor, so he told them to have that derogatory junk removed from the schools. Well, he and other people made noises; it has been removed throughout the years. That is what prompted me to do something, so I worked and created beauty so my children will see that it was not all bad. The more I created, the more I wanted to do it. Some coincidence, isn't it? In my spiritual thinking, I think it is a plan beyond my comprehension.

You described writing as therapy in your autobiography. In what ways was writing a form of therapy?

In my thirties, I was having a difficult time, especially with my husband, who was a womanizer. There were in-law problems and other personal problems. Writing became a natural expression, a way of putting my thoughts in a positive manner.

You have also written that "The women in [your] community have helped a lot," especially your Kivu (mother). How have the women in your life, past and present, helped you?

Women became my friends because of difficulties. They helped in a lot of ways. Talking with women at any age is good. They offer advice. We end up laughing at our problems. Kivu was my mother-in-law. We became close after I showed her my bruises, otherwise hidden before. Another old lady told me to do this. I worked hard at earning her love. She finally voiced it, and loved me more than her children.

In your poem "Near Mountains, Waters and Trees," Eskasoni is a place of renewal. In the same poem, you make particular mention of the Eskasoni Women's Auxiliary. It's interesting the way you bring together Eskasoni as a place of healing, and the centrality of the women's community there. Is there a strong community of women in Eskasoni that is important to you?

In Eskasoni, there is a powerful group of women who try with all their abilities to have a good place to live. I know it is not perfect, but peaceful. Sometimes we are unable to control certain things, but I see so much goodness, more good than bad. This past week we had three deaths because of sickness. I saw men fix up the houses where a wake will be held. Women help to clean, and they comfort. The choir which sang ancient hymns that Mrs. Annie Cremo used to sing. The choir, who are some of them young, sang the very difficult worded hymn just perfect for Mrs. Cremo, the fiddler.

How much contact do you have with other Aboriginal women writers in Atlantic Canada? Who is your community of writers?

My contact with Native writers is constant. They ask for advice, etc. In the past, teachers, nuns, and elderly women became my advisors. Correct cultural advice was important to me. Being a foster child is not like learning along with family members. Yet I remember every detail of the little time I had with my own family.

My own people have given me the most encouragement, but also teachers, professors and other writers.

Your writing stresses the need to claim your own voice, your own perspective. How is this related to your role as a writer?

When I claim my voice, it is the language, not others writing about us. If it is my perspective, it comes from the core. I teach what I know. Healing for others and challenging cultural stereotypes give me strength. The importance, to me, is keeping the cultural values alive. In Eskasoni, most of the people speak Mi'kmaq, and in the classroom, a problem is more easily explained in Mi'kmaq.

Besides being a means of healing and teaching, you have also portrayed writing poems as a process of recording. I'm thinking of your poem "Aunt Harriet's Waltes," for example. What is being recorded?

Recording, to me, means showing, teaching, explaining. In "Aunt Harriet's Waltes," there was no wrong being done. It was Shrove Tuesday and they were playing the last card game. The jackpot was the dime, as you remember. Aunt Harriet was a sweet old lady who had a hunchback, the broken back cured years earlier with herbal medicine. It took her years to walk upright. To me, it was a great crime to punish her. She died in 1985. Her back was broken in 1909 — no doctors or hospitals then. Herbal medicine helped her. To spare the humiliation of her going to court, her fourteen-year-old daughter went and paid a $25 fine. The waltes, by the way, was seized by the Mounties and is now at the RCMP Archives. The ancient game rightly belongs to her only daughter, Mrs. Susie Marshall of Eskasoni.

Your poems sometimes extend invitations. "The Art of Communica-

tion" is one example of this. *Why is it important to you to extend these invitations to your readers?*

In "The Art of Communication," you can see that I am trying to communicate. When you come to my home, I will speak your language. I will do everything in my power to make you comfortable. Remember, that was written in 1988, not too long ago, but the racist attitude was still there. Subtle, but nevertheless still there. The cry for help is there. In high school, I was still a child, but was expected to be brave and fight the battlefield of assimilation. As you can see, I was asking for help. I speak for the Native children, and for minorities.

You also communicate through legends, in some poems. Your use of Glooscap comes to mind, for example. Can you talk about why legends are significant in your writing?

Legends spoken by my people are examples of teaching something to a child: a moral value, something sacred, like a teaching cartoon. The word "Glooscap" may have come from the Mi'kmaw saying Ki'sulkip, meaning the one who made us. Missionaries meant well, but their explanations were not always correct.

What other sources of poetic inspiration are important to you?

There are many sources of poetic inspiration. At first, my poems were to teach the non-Native about our way of life. Later, I wrote about anything that moved my spirit. I was hesitant to write about spirituality. Now I am more open about it. It surprises me at times when there is a comment about it.

What is the connection between spirituality and writing?

The connection in my writing about spirituality is based on my dependence on inner voice, a gut feeling, coincidences, dreams interpreted. Spirituality, a part of inner voice in one's soul has to be there to tap if one wants to write about it; the aloneness of my creativeness has been done because the making of word pictures gets harder and harder. Or is it easy because the spiritual part I find more a part of me than anything else? Every part of my life revolves around the positive; if I dwell on the negative for even a short time, I feel awful. As you see, the soul-searching part, "Am I doing the right thing?" is always with me no matter what I write about. Before I create even a two-liner I ask for help. When done, I give thanks. My story continues. Also acknowledging *Kisulkw* (The One who made us), *Sesos* (Jesus), *Niksam* (God) in my writing helps. I am never shy about that part because it is the truth.

What do you think of when you think of place? Your own home?

Eskasoni? Cape Breton? The whole earth?

When I think of a place it can be a wigwam, our home in Whycocomagh, the many apartments Frank and I lived in with our children. Now my beautiful home in Eskasoni and, no matter where on earth I go, I am happy to come home to Cape Breton. Of course, my final home is important. I know in my heart it will be beautiful. I listen to the beatitudes and feel good. I even think of a shelter we lived in, a root cellar when our home was repaired. The roof had burned, so there were major repairs. My mom and dad and my sister stayed in that root cellar as comfortable as possible. I know how to be poor, so adaptation is easy for me.

Your poem "Whycocomagh" expresses deep grief over a lost home. Can you talk about the experiences behind the poem?

In "Whycocomagh," my whole world was one of love and security and being part of a family life. Indifference was part of my life after leaving the place until I got married. That is why I never wanted separation ever again from my husband. Abandon my children? No way. Security is like, welded into my brain. I stood any injustice to keep my children together.

You have written of great pain and personal loss — of a brother and sister and other family members. How have these things affected you?

The great loss of my family members made me a lonely orphan. It made commitment important to my well-being. If you are not honest with me, I never forget. It took me a long time to accept cheatings by my husband. One day I went berserk and smashed our car to bits. But I felt good later, asserting myself. Though the damage hurt us, my husband understood. Some people can take so much.

You have overcome many obstacles in your life. What are the greatest challenges facing Aboriginal women writers?

The greatest difficulties facing Native women writers is that they are shy and have low self-esteem. I did at first but got braver as time went on. The applause is what boosted my spirit. My knees were trembling but sang after speaking. Our audiences are mostly non-Native. That alone bends your shadow. Once I read a review that someone wrote; it made me mad, and I promised myself I'd make her eat her words, and I thought, "Remember, this is our second language." I just do the best I can and hope that it is received as education, as something that should be taught.

What women poets, Native or non-Native, do you admire most?

Maxine Tynes moves my heart. Pauline Johnson is the first one

I admired because she told the truth. There are just too many; I may have liked some things they wrote, but not all of their work. There are some good, some bad. I hate reading negative stuff. If followed by positive, it is all right. Part of my life has been negative, but I hate dwelling on it.

Thank you for teaching me more about your writing and your culture.

Hope this is enough. If not, ask for more.

Yours truly, Rita Joe

Lesley-Anne Bourne, Poet of Lakes

"When I first came to Prince Edward Island, I missed lakes so much. I still do. I don't like salt water. I like lakes, clear water. They're quiet, beautiful. I mean, the ocean beaches here are stunning, but I get there and all I want is Muskoka, or Lake Nipissing. I like this beautiful east coast, but for me, it isn't as good as a lake. A lake is probably my metaphor."

photo: Tom MacDonald

Lesley-Anne Bourne grew up in North Bay, Ontario. She studied creative writing at York University and the University of British Columbia. Lesley-Anne is the author of three collections of poetry: The Story of Pears *(Penumbra, 1990),* Skinny Girls *(Penumbra, 1993) and* Field Day *(Penumbra, 1996). She has also published a novel,* The Bubble Star *(The Porcupine's Quill, 1998). For the past decade, Lesley-Anne has lived in Charlottetown, where she teaches creative writing at the University of Prince Edward Island. Her literary awards include the Bliss Carman Award, the Air Nova Poetry Award, and the Air Canada Award.*

Lesley-Anne and I talked in Beanz Café in Charlottetown.

Isn't it unusual for an author under the age of thirty-five to have published three books of poetry?

I hadn't thought about it until we planned to talk, that I'd written three books in six years. I don't recommend it. I had really written so much, so fast. It felt like I had to achieve so much.

What were some of your earliest experiences as a writer?

At school, Mrs. Desjardins asked us to write a poem, so I wrote a poem. It was about the fall, leaves glowing like precious gems. Maybe in grade seven, it's okay to be clichéd. I don't remember anyone teaching me to write poetry. By high school, my poems were in the yearbook, which was horrifying. I think because my parents didn't know that much about my writing because I didn't show them, they were threatened by it and a little scared of it. Maybe they thought it was making me unhappy; if anything, it was a way of dealing with things.

You have workshopped with numerous writers, including Don Coles, Katherine Govier, Lorna Crozier, Phyllis Webb, Matt Cohen and Eli Mandel. But b.p. nichol seems to have been an absolutely key mentor for you. What do you think is his importance, for you?

I had seen b.p. nichol read at the Northern Writers' Guild meeting. He was such a larger-than-life guy. I'd never heard sound poetry, and he spit on me because I was close to him, and I thought I was going to die. (laughs) Sometimes he's present in my head in a way I never would have expected. Now I understand a lot of things he did and told me back then. He would make me write on a huge sheet of paper the size of a table, and I hated that. There are times I can hear him saying, "If you wrote it, you'd be done with it." I think I call on him a lot when I'm in doubt.

What about women literary mentors?

Lorna Crozier was one of the first women poets I got to work with, at Banff. It was such a relief to show my work to her. I'd been showing poetry to men for years. I'd been working on "Celebration," and in it, the voice of the poem is talking about her mother throwing a little juice glass when the mother is really frustrated, and at home with two girls. I thought, "Who is going to care about this?" Lorna thought there was really something there. I didn't necessarily get that response from Don or b.p. I think Lorna opened a whole other area for me to write about. Getting your period, sex in the back of a car. And I think she made it okay for readers to enjoy poetry. I still think we try and classify women poets, and what women write about, in a way that we don't for male poets.

I also worked with Phyllis Webb. She was like the high priestess. At Banff, I read a poem that had a lot of ice and water and glass. Phyllis Webb said, "What is Lesley-Anne saying in this poem?" Nobody said anything. Phyllis said to me, "Perhaps you don't want to be heard." I started thinking, "Why the hell would you write if you didn't want somebody to know what you were writing about?" You have to take a risk and let somebody hear what you're writing about, or what's the point? I'm sure she booted me ahead by years. That was a huge turning point for me.

Do you consider yourself a feminist poet?

Yes. When I started publishing, I made sure I put my name as "Lesley-Anne," even though all my family and friends called me

"Lesley," "Les." I wanted people to know it was a woman's voice and a woman's experience.

You have workshopped extensively, and now you teach creative writing. How do the workshops you've been teaching affect your own writing habits?

The workshops I'm teaching mostly affect my creative process in a good way, but I do find it hard to write when I'm teaching full-time. My pattern is to get a lot of writing done in June, July and August. The workshops force me to be more outgoing than I really am. They force me to talk; sometimes you don't know what you think about something until you say it. Workshops force you to have three hours a week where you're thinking about writing, and not just your own, which is a really good thing.

You use popular culture in your poems quite a bit: song lyrics, references to Sleeman's beer and things like that. Why is that important to you?

It's important that people know what poets are wearing, what they're drinking. Popular culture influences everything. I used to joke that I was going to write "the retail poems" (laughs) because I had a lot of retail experience. I have had arguments with people who say that poetry and popular culture should be separate. Good luck.

Your first book, The Story of Pears, *contains a lot of northern Ontario landscapes. Is* Pears *a northern book?*

I'm sure it's a northern book. It's definitely the northern Ontario landscape: trees, granite, lakes, all the things I miss here. Someone asked me to write a poem for a fairly big national anthology. It had to be a Maritime-type poem. I couldn't do it. For a year, I tried to write about the sea in a way that wasn't clichéd. I can't do it, but I could give you twenty-five poems about lakes. (laughs)

In a poem called "Arctic Faces," the speaker says that if she squints at the ocean, she'd see a lake. What does that mean?

That's my one Maritime poem. It's about my sister leaving, and leaving me in the Maritimes – Pictou, where the ferry is. I remember thinking, "I actually wrote a Maritime poem!" — although it's all about squinting and turning it all into Ontario. (laughs)

You seem to layer landscapes, maybe increasingly so. Some poems in Field Day, *like "Coral Negro," layer Cuba with northern Ontario. What is happening there?*

That is me trying to turn the whole world into Ontario. The

poem starts in Cuba, or Pictou Landing, and I drag it, kicking and screaming, back to Muskoka, to my cottage, to North Bay.

You've written about family relationships a lot. Is that difficult?

My family is always surprised by how much I remember. Details – my sister feeding me spaghetti out of garbage cans. (laughs) I think they're surprised at how much I've salvaged or dug up or saved out of the junk of what's happened to us. I think that's what most writers are doing. That's why it's hard to have a sibling or family member who is writing. You are revealing a part of them that maybe you have no right to reveal.

The relationships between women in your poems are interesting: mothers and daughters, but sisters and women friends, too. Often these poems seem to suggest the gap between women. I'm thinking of the lines "I miss her/like a lake" in your poem "Burning Lake." Interesting how the woman and the landscape seem inextricable...

That poem was about the poet Laura Lush. She and I are so close; I think we egg each other on to write about lakes. I like writing about sister relationships.

How do you think your work has evolved?

My first two books were very naïve. *Field Day* asks a lot more questions. I think in the previous two books, I was just trying to answer questions. The first two books were "snapshots," I think.

Where is your writing community?

I don't have a writing community here, male or female. Richard and I write, but we rarely have time to talk about writing. I think I came here and didn't fit in because I'm younger than some of the other women who are writing and, for various reasons, I didn't fit in. I'm shy and find it so hard to come to new places. I don't have women writers here who I show my work to, though I have shown my fiction to Deirdre Kessler. Laura Lush in Toronto is the person I send my poems to after I've written them. I do a lot of email communication with other writers. Sue Goyette is close [Halifax], but not close enough.

Carmelita McGrath's New World

"I think you have to challenge the myths if you're a woman and you're writing, because in the official versions, we're not part of history."

photo: Manfred Bucheit

Carmelita McGrath was born in Branch, Newfoundland, in 1960. Her books are Poems on Land and Water *(Killick, 1992),* Walking to Shenak *(Killick, 1994), and* To the New World *(Killick, 1997). Carmelita co-edited* Their Lives and Times: Women in Newfoundland and Labrador, A Collage *(Killick, 1995), and edited* Signatures *(Killick, 1996), an anthology of writing and visual art. Carmelita has also published poems in numerous journals including* TickleAce, Event, The Fiddlehead, The Journey Prize Anthology *and* Room of One's Own. *She has won seven Newfoundland and Labrador Arts and Letters awards for poetry and fiction. Carmelita lives in St. John's. I talked with her there.*

How did coming from an outport impact on you?

One of the things that is important, that drives me, is that I was almost always outdoors — a very expansive, open, outdoor world. Lots of sea, green hills. The community itself is in a deep valley. Big rivers. It was a place to live in the world, and not hide away from it. I spent a lot of my life as a child outside, absorbing what was around. It was also extremely isolated at the time. It's not isolated now; I can get in my car and go there in less than two hours. We had dirt roads, and we never owned a car. I can remember as a child seeing lights across the bay and probably noticing that for the first time — probably because that's about when these communities got electricity, in the mid-sixties. I remember seeing the lights and thinking "I wonder what's over there," so it was very closed off from everywhere else. It was hard to imagine what everywhere else was like.

There are less than 300 there now. It lost a lot with the de-
cline in the fisheries. It was almost 100 percent a fishing town. A
lot of subsistence farming, too. The place always smelled like fish.
Did you study Newfoundland poets in school?
Very little. Pratt was all we had for awhile. It was very weird.
It wasn't that people weren't writing or publishing; but it was what
was in the schools. It wasn't until the seventies that anthologies of
Newfoundland writing were being published, by Breakwater, among
others. There was a big boom. In high school I got access to other
writers from here. I remember reading a poem by Helen Porter,
and it sounded so real to me. There was something so familiar in
what she was saying. It was how she knew certain phrases and rhythms
that I was familiar with — even though she was from St. John's,
and I was from St. Mary's Bay. I remember reading Des Walsh's
poetry, and thinking, "You actually can do it here — where have
these people been all my life?" It was a kind of Newfoundland pa-
triotism. The blossoming in the seventies happened in theatre, too.
Since the nineties, I've noticed a big explosion of people pub-
lishing their work, and a new generation. I know a lot of writers
now around my own age, and I didn't once. There are things like
the Burning Rock Collective, and groups like that. It's not just
new writing; it's writing from a new perspective..
When did your earliest literary endeavours take place?
In elementary school, I was an editor of the school newspaper.
I guess I got identified with writing at that time. I remember some-
body coming to the house and asking me to write a letter to some
government department for her, you know? I was only about twelve.
(laughs) In a small community, some people were the drawing guys,
some other people were associated with music, or being able to
shoe a horse or whatever. Everybody has a skill.
When did you first publish a poem as an adult?
I was about twenty four. It was in *TickleAce.* I was between
leaving teaching high school and trying to figure out what else to
do. Then I met a poet in St. John's. He said there's this workshop
group I might be interested in. The workshop was really frighten-
ing to join because there were so many experienced writers in
there. I was thinking, "I don't want to read my poems aloud with
Percy Janes in the room" (laughs) — he was a hero of mine, as a
teenager. It was a great group to be part of. Roberta Buchanan
was in it, and Paul Bowdring. We used to call it the Thursday
Collective.

In Arc, *in a relatively recent review of three new anthologies of Canadian poetry, Mary Dalton wrote about the exclusion of Newfoundland writing from discourse about Canadian poetry. Why do you think this exclusion tends to happen?*

I wonder if often, anthologists don't think of Newfoundland as part of Canada. Maybe the exclusion is just not ever thinking of us. We're part of a political arrangement with Canada, but culturally? I often feel very, very separate. I think there is also the anthologists' laziness. In order to approach a place like this and see what's going on in the literature, you'd have to crash through so many stereotypes. I'm sure that central Canada, when they think of Newfoundland, they think of humour. So if you can throw humour at them, they can accept it, because it's part of the stereotype they have. But if you bring them something different, they don't really know what to do with it.

Your latest book, To The New World, *explores newness, origins, sites of creation. What themes were you exploring in the poems?*

I was thinking a lot about origins, roots, where things begin. Cycles. It was almost a physical thing. I started working on this book when I was pregnant. I started thinking of her [my daughter] as a world coming into being. I was reading a lot of history, science, a lot that had to do with origins, with creation, but also with the end of things — how things come apart and are destroyed. There were a lot of things going on during the writing of that book — everything from the birth to the cod moratorium to the Cabot extravaganza. Having a child was a new way of being, for me. It was much more focused, and time was different. With the word "To" in the book's title, I was also toasting the new world.

There is a strong focus, in To The New World, *on women from different generations. Why?*

A lot of that was an attempt to link my daughter with her past. Not that that was conscious, but it was definitely going on. Who is this new person? She is herself, but is also linked to all these generations in various ways, not just genetically, but through history.

There are numerous journeys in the poems — for instance, the women coming over from Ireland and other places, to Newfoundland, the journey of the unborn child. How did these journeys get into the poems?

Thinking of a child as an explorer was fun; there are so many possibilities in that image. Being born is sort of like landing and claiming the territory for — what? Not for king and country, but for yourself. It was enjoyable to find images and embed them.

There are quite a few matrilineal connections in your writing. I'm thinking of the poem "City of Second Chances" in your book Poems on Land and Water. *There you have written about the scrub-woman's granddaughter. Why is it important to you to tell these women's stories?*

I thought a lot about the hardships of women while I was writing. I also thought about all of their dreams, wishes. The things that really keep them going. One person I had in mind when I was writing it [*To the New World*] was one of the grandmothers the book was dedicated to, Fanny. She was the midwife for the whole community for generations, and grew up extremely poor. She had eleven kids, and took care of her own birthing. She was a fiercely strong woman, and the image I had of her was, after her hard life, sitting in a rocking chair with a cigarette hanging out of her mouth, and a Western novel in her hand — being utterly worn out, but content. I wanted this book to have more of a sense of that than all of the trouble and hardship.

In both of your books, desire, aspiration, seem gendered. What I mean is, you've written about women struggling, women whose desires reflect the ideology of capitalist culture — like having a fur coat.

A lot of the desires revolve around consumerism. I come from a working-class background. You have to get that consumer thing in order to reject it. The women in "City of Second Chances" were at that phase of getting it.

In To The New World, *you describe birth as "a search for the other." Is writing poetry a kind of search for the "other," too?*

Oh, yeah. It's a chance to inhabit other beings, to not be who you are. If you concentrate hard enough, you can be that tree out there. It is a chance to get outside the trap of having only one body and one life.

You use explorer-type journals in To The New World, *too. They sound very convincing. How did you do such a good job of appropriating that kind of objective, male discourse, right down to its syntax, its tone of constant qualification?*

I spent a lot of time in archives, reading journal documents. In each one of those, the wording is based on the sequence and rhythm of an actual piece of text. But the words are mine, they're not real. It's fun because you're writing in one voice, inhabiting one type of body, but then you get to step outside yourself and recreate another voice. You're almost a different body; it's different hands writing it when you're doing that.

What is the relationship between the "journal" headers and the poems that follow them?

I wrote the journals after I wrote the poems. These specific ones were tailored for the poems that go underneath them.

In one of your poems, you write, "[N]o one knows a true thing about John Cabot, or where he landed." Is poetry, for you, also about exploding cultural myths?

I think so. If I had one image of Cabot, while I was writing that, I could see him on a dirty street, a dirty little boy sailing a leaf-boat. That's probably about as close to the truth as anything, because Cabot is someone we've made up. We've taken a real person nobody knows very much about and made up this sort of myth that has to do, among other things, with tourism. I think you have to challenge the myths if you're a woman and you're writing, because in the official versions, we're not part of history. For example, Fanny, who gave birth to the community, who in a way created a new world — Fanny will never become a cultural hero, or all those women who made the cooking utensils pristinely clean so no one got poisoned. And even now, who gives awards for raising children? To me, uncelebrated creation acts are important. In making the child the explorer, I'm pushing that what the child sees is important. Children are impressed by what women do, often. They explore that world first.

I also find that often when these women are recreated from a male poet's point of view, they are too solemn, too stoic, too heroic. They have no flaws. Men have this great desire, in their writing, to create good women. Redeeming women. I don't think the women I write about that are really like that. They are heroic, in ways, but they are also people with all kinds of flaws. They do get roped into consumerism, and all kinds of things — bad deals, bad marriages.

The last poem in To the New World *contains a reference to "the dappled truth." Interesting image to end a collection with. Do you want to comment on that?*

I didn't want to end the book with any sort of assurance, I suppose. (laughs) I wanted to go out of the book as if I were going somewhere else.

Heather Browne Prince and the Gift of Place

"What you're handed from 'your place' — Fredericton, or wherever — that's the gift. Part of breaking through the surface of things is recognizing that gift. You can't ever turn your back on the richness of your own world, or you've lost everything."

photo: Stanya © P.M.A.

Heather Browne Prince lives in Sussex Corner, New Brunswick. She studied creative writing at the University of British Columbia. Heather is a member of the Wolf Tree Writers group in Fredericton; she has also worked with the Fredericton Women's Theatre Collective. A writer of short stories and poems, Heather is the author of two collections of poetry: Knowledge in the Hands *(Goose Lane, 1994) and* Where Water and Gravel Meet *(Owl's Head, 1998). Her poetry has appeared in a number of anthologies, including* Poetic Voices of the Maritimes; The Windhorse Reader: Choice Poems of '94; *and* Vintage '91: Prize-Winning Poems from the League of Canadian Poets. *I talked with Heather in the house where she grew up in Sussex, New Brunswick.*

Can you talk about your earliest experiences as a writer?

As a child, I had little Campfire notebooks that I would write in. After I filled them, they went out into the garbage and got burned, because I knew how private they were, knew words had power and effect. And they scared me to death! I wasn't going to let anybody else into them because they were going to get into me if they did, you know? I think writers are very private.

But, obviously, you "came out," at some point — or I wouldn't be here.

(laughs) I suppose I did. It took a very long time. I suppose it was after the study of silence, because out of silence comes voice. So then I decided "Yes, I'm going to be heard." But that was a long odyssey.

What form did your study of silence take?

I went to a monastery in Rogersville and worked for a week without speaking, without anyone talking to me. Then I followed that up at UBC for a bit. I have to be very quiet to write. But at some point, you want to be heard, you want to become visible.

Was deciding to be heard a joyful experience? A frightening one?

It's a crossing-over point. It's almost as large as discovering a place where water and gravel meet. Once you open up, and once you put it down on paper, it's there, and it's very frightening. And I think the only reason you would ever do it is because people like Kent Thompson and Nancy Bauer said, "Yes, you can, this is valid, your story is alright, you're alright." There's many people to consider. If you're writing about something as simple as home, you realize that you're revealing your mother's illnesses, your father's incapacities, and so on. It's a huge consideration.

How has belonging to the Wolf Tree Writers group enhanced the process of "going public"?

It gave us a stamp of visibility. Margaret [McLeod] and Shari [Andrews] and I have been working together since about '83. About two years ago, we said, "Let's put a name on this, let's get out there." It's a group of women going public, saying "We've got something to say."

What kind of affirmation did the more formal workshops at UNB and UBC provide?

At the Maritime Writers Workshop in '83 or thereabouts, Patrick Lane put one of his poems on the chalkboard and asked us why it was a poem. The different responses from each person made me realize "I'm not thinking like person A, B, or C, I'm thinking very differently," yet recognizing that my thinking was okay, too. I think it's that affirmation, to use your term, that you as an individual are singular and correct, and that there isn't a right or a wrong. People need to be told that. Also, it was important to recognize that there is a family of people who love to write, and they are your family in a very special way.

You have written a long poem sequence called "A White Gift" in your book Knowledge in the Hands. *Can you tell me what the "white gift" is, and where it came from?*

The white gift was an egg that my grandfather offered me when I was a child. This was in my memory. Even as a child, you recognize how important it is when someone gives you such a gift, how important you are to that very tall man handing you this thing,

145

rubbing the egg on his sleeve, that twinkle in his eye. You know something's up. You try to remember this, as an adult, try to mark it and make it mean.

"A White Gift" is put together in an organic, associative way. It doesn't seem to follow a linear pattern. Is this an accurate characterization of the poem's form, do you think?

I think so. It took about nine months to write, an interesting number. It was a very hard time, punctuated by a lot of time in which there wasn't writing. At the time, I was anti-classical; I was trying to put classical form in a place where I could learn from it and use it, and then smash it and use it. I was also struggling with open verse. I didn't know where I was, as a writer. I wasn't in either camp. And yet I had a huge welling-up of feeling for the organic. I think I believed in my heart during the writing that that was where I was coming from, that I couldn't be something I was not — which was my great reverence for classical form. I was also wrestling with people, very erudite people in my writing world who had a great capacity for expressing themselves. I recognized in my own world that there was just this great silence and time without words, and inability to express things. And so, out of that real life came the reason for so much punctuation, so much white space. It's a huge belief that the word was never going to do it anyway, kind of a Beckett sense. It was all a wrestling match.

Physical gestures, however small, seem important to you. Why does gesture, or, as you put it, "a mime of being" matter to you?

It's a body language, a gesture, a silence, and a punctuation of the word with silence. It's rubbing your nose — like this. That's real. The rest of it is just a mime. "Only occasionally do we break through the surface of things." I think that's what I was starting to realize.

Your poems contain an interesting blend of metaphorical, "literary" language and vernacular language. Does this observation correspond in any way with your sense of your own poetic language?

Yes. I think "A White Gift" was the first time I realized the vernacular is important, that where I come from and what I hear in my part of the world is okay — for instance, when my grandfather says, "It's time to be getting in." What you're handed from "your place" — Fredericton, or wherever — that's the gift. And if you turn your back on it, if you think your gift hasn't been quite as great as the next person's gift, then you're doing a great harm to that gift. Part of breaking through the surface of things is recognizing that gift. It takes awhile.

Why is "your part of the world," or place, important to you?

Place is extremely important. Seamus Heaney said, in a poem called "Fosterling," that it took him fifty years to see what was right in front of him. And yet, for those fifty years, he was writing about his father out in the garden, and what the people were saying, and so on. It took him a long time to wake up to the fact that this was what he was writing about, this was where he was coming from.

If I didn't have this home — "home" in the larger sense — what would I write about? I have no idea. But it takes an incredible amount of self-confidence and time writing to make me believe that what I have under my nose is good enough. No one can ever tell you that and make you see it! You have to learn that yourself. I have always thought the richness of the dialect, of what I hear here, has always been absolutely wonderful. Then the horror was going away to university, and finding out that what I respected, and the milieu that I grew up in was not the only little container of the world, that there was another world, and perhaps these two didn't quite merge. University slowed me down, as far as my writing was concerned, because my worlds were colliding. I became silent again, because I didn't think my particular world was rich enough compared to this new academic world I was introduced to. I became quiet until I looked around for a while. (laughs) But you can't ever turn your back on the richness or your own world, or you've lost everything.

The importance of place is suggested in your heavy use of prepositions. Your poems contain many references to "in," "under," "beside," and so on — references to "where." Is poetry a process of situating, for you?

There has been a lot of situating going on. That was something I wasn't aware of, in the writing. When I wrote *Where Water and Gravel Meet*, I said, "Hey, that's the place I've been looking for." I returned there a hundred times, to that juncture between a gravelly place, something solid, and something fluid and rolling. You're absolutely right; there's been this positioning.

The landscapes in your poems also show an interest in how things are constructed, in architectural details like doorways, fireplaces, buildings. You've written a poem about building a fireplace, for example. Is this somehow related to the creative process?

Yes — deciding what detail you are going to pick. I like your term "architectural selection." If it hadn't been for writing the fireplace poem, and realizing that the construction of a poem and the construction of a fireplace are very similar, starting from the ground up, like the lineation in that poem ... I think that was the first poem in which I became vertical, in the writing, rather than horizontal — it was the fireplace going up! I remember fighting with these little short lines. (laughs)

Besides the Wolf Tree Writers, who is your literary community in Atlantic Canada?

It tends to be localized, for me. There's a community of writers in Fredericton. If I'm having a reading, I know Travis Lane is going to be in the audience, or Nancy Bauer. When I launched my first book, Kent Thompson and his wife came across on the ferry from Nova Scotia. Fred Cogswell was there. Fred and I probably communicate once a week, about writing. As far as the rest of the Atlantic region, Mary Dalton was a stranger; then she reviewed my work, then I heard her at Word on the Street. Richard Lemm will send me a note when he sees my work in a journal. So it's that kind of "knowing by extension." (laughs) And then, of course, there's the Writers' Federation of New Brunswick and the Sussex Writers and Illustrators Group (SWIG). It's that kind of family extension.

What has been your greatest joy as a writer?

What a terrific question. When I went to my twenty-fifth high school reunion, I refused to go in and ask, "What are you doing?" or "How many children do you have?" My question was, "What's your love?" (laughs) I got responses like "sunshine and green grass." My greatest joy? I think, finally, achieving understanding. Writing, for me, is process, always process. Product isn't all that important. But at some point, all of a sudden I understand where water and gravel meet, what it means, what I'm trying to unravel. So the joy is knowledge.

Agnes Walsh and the Old Country of the Heart

"I've always been preoccupied with the same subjects. Aloneness. Language. Place. The loss of language. I think more about 'place' than 'region.' Maybe it's some of my anger that does that. If things are called 'regional,' then why isn't this place [Newfoundland] part of all that regional stuff they're always talking about, up there, you know, in Canada? I don't think about the other 'regions'; I really only write from this place. I love writing about place."

photo: Ed Kavanagh

Agnes Walsh was born and grew up in Placentia, Newfoundland. She has worked in professional theatre for over twenty years in St. John's. She was co-founder of Neighbourhood Dance Works, a modern dance company that now sponsers an annual festival of modern dance in St. John's. Writing since the age of ten, her first love is poetry. Her collection of poems In the Old Country of My Heart *was published by Killick Press in 1996. Her work appears in many literary journals, such as* TickleAce *and* Pottersfield Portfolio, *as well in the anthologies* 31 Newfoundland Poets *and* Newfoundland Poets Volume 1, *and* Signatures: Newfoundland Women Artists and Writers. *In* The Old Country of My Heart *is presently being considered for translation by the prestigious Camoes Institute in Lisbon, Portugal. Agnes has read her work in the United States and across Canada, and recently toured Portugal and Ireland with her work. She is currently working on a new manuscript of poetry as well as scripting a novel into a play and also co-writing a new play.*

I talked with Agnes in her kitchen overlooking St. John's harbour.

Was the military base at Placentia a big presence in your life?

Very big. I have three sisters who married Americans and went there; I married an American when I was sixteen and went there. Almost all the friends I had growing up are somewhere in the United States.

What about in terms of your writing?

I was really lucky. I met an American serviceman who worked for Naval Intelligence. My book of poems is dedicated to him: Thomas Joseph James Bonfiglio III. Some people think it's some sixteenth-century Italian poet, or something. (laughs) He was an American sailor from Brooklyn, New York, who I met in a snack bar in Placentia. I went over to the juke box and played a song; this guy, sitting at the counter said, "So, you like Bob Dylan, do you?" I said, "If that's him, yeah." So me and Tom Bonfiglio started talking. I told him I loved poetry more than anything in the world. He mentioned all these Beat poets, like Ferlinghetti. There was a library on the base, and he couldn't take the books out, but he copied all these poems out by long-hand — not only the Beat poets, but other poets I couldn't get my hands on — our library was so small – only Yeats, Wordsworth. Eventually, I showed him some of my work. He was really encouraging. I was about fifteen at the time; he was nineteen. We both quit high school because we were bored. He joined the military. I met him again later when I went to the States, when I was nineteen; he had changed so much. I can't track him down now.

What poets became important to you?

The poets Tom Bonfiglio introduced me to, the Beat poets. Beat poetry helped give me the guts to say what I wanted to say. The Beat poets told me it was okay to be angry, you know? So the injustices here in Newfoundland could come out, thanks to them. The same time as I was reading the Beats, I was babysitting for these American people on the base. They left me with their record collection, incredible jazz. I was thirteen years old, listening to John Coltrane and Nina Simone and Billie Holiday. No wonder I was bored to death in school, learning that cars were made in Detroit and stuff like that. I couldn't wait until three o'clock to go down and baby-sit, and listen to John Coltrane and Miles Davis and all these people. That was my education.

Did you study any Newfoundland poets in school at all?

Oh God, no. Absolutely nothing. I read, and talked to some grade eleven students the other day about how I was educated. I said, "I hope you're getting a better education than I did, because all schools did to me was beat me away from their doors." We were made fun of, the way we talked, because we were from the bay, and a lot of our teachers were from St. John's. They were constantly trying to correct our speech. So anything to do with

Newfoundland was worthless — it wasn't allowed at all. There was no Newfoundland history. I mean, I just took a course at the university so that I could learn something about Newfoundland's political history.

What was your earliest writing like?

I was writing every day since I was about ten. I was such an idealist — I would see something on TV about the Civil Rights movement in the States, and I would write a poem about it. I was really affected by the plight of Black people in the States. My writing was very gushing about the injustices of the world.

And after that?

When I went away to the States, I did book reviews. When I came back to Newfoundland in 1977, I went looking for the writers and theatre people. I was fortunate enough to meet Des Walsh, a local poet. We were all crammed in this taxi out at Mount Pearl, or somewhere, and I pulled some poems out of my pocket and said, "Do you want to read some?" He read them and said he wanted to publish them in an anthology called *Thirty-One Newfoundland Poets*. That opened up a lot for me. It was the same with *In the Old Country of My Heart*; Ed Kavanagh [from Killick Press] was after me for years to get those poems together. Finally, he had to sit down with me; I was too scattered, with writing for theatre and taking care of two children.

Your work seems deeply concerned with issues of language and power. Take the example of the teacher "correcting" your speech in school. Is that, for you, a form of colonization?

It definitely is. Seamus Heaney calls it "the government of the tongue." There's nothing worse than someone telling you to shut up, that you don't speak right, or that their language is superior to yours. We're not the only place to suffer under that. But in the place I came from, we all understood each other.

But where does that place you, as a poet? In your poem, "The Time that Passes," a mother warns her daughter/poet: "But you watch it, my mother said, /it's your tongue too that was dipped/in the blue ink, and do go leaking iambics/all the day long." What does that warning mean for the daughter/poet?

As I say in that poem, we've been "educated into ignorance." For some people, I think a lot of education is a really bad thing, even though I know that sounds a bit strange. For me, it would be a really bad thing. I remember having tea with a woman who came from where I did, and who became a social worker. I remember thinking how much her speech had changed. She would say, like, "Shall we *do* lunch?" I can't stand it. I wanted to say to my friend, "What happened to the way you used to talk?" It's not that you have to stay that way and never learn, but why should your language have been coated over? I have to watch myself, If you listen to the CBC all the time, you'll end up talking like them. (laughs) It scares me. I have to turn it off sometimes, and turn on some really bad local radio station and hear the dialects — now, if only they'd say something interesting (laughs) with that accent, it would be wonderful.

Spoken language seems to be important to you?

Very, very important. Both my parents had very little education; I think they only got as far as third grade or something. They had to help with the fish or the garden. Education was only for people who were going to be nuns or priests, teachers or nurses. My mother and father are both very bright people. And their memory … I know it comes from not reading a lot. My mother can remember things from when she was three years old, the way a piece of lace was blowing in a window, things like that. Exactly what the weather was like in 1918. It's a different way of thinking. I had a ballad writer in my family, but he wasn't a "writer"; he wrote ballads in his head, and sang them. They stayed alive that way. There was always theatre in these small communities, too; when you got bored, you got together and told stories. There was music and dancing at the end of the night.

What things preoccupy you as a poet?

I've always been preoccupied with the same subjects. Aloneness. Language. Place. The loss of language. My new book deals with the early settlement of Placentia Bay and the migration over from Ireland to Newfoundland. The old political anger comes up again, as I research things that were done to the Irish and then the Newfoundland people. Maybe the same things that made me angry when I was young, watching the Civil Rights movement events on TV, all those injustices. Those things will always run through my work.

You work in theatre, too. Does theatre allow for a more overtly political message than poetry?

I think there is as much room, in poetry, for politics, as there is in theatre. The only thing I'm nervous about is that in theatre, you can put something in someone's face; in poetry, if you do that, you're preaching, almost. The first poem in *Old Country,* "The

Time that Passes," is extremely political. But I try to bring it back to something more personal, and I try to make fun of myself in it, too. You can get away with more in theatre, verbally; you can say a lot more. But there are also political poets who can say things politically, in poems, better than I can.

"The Time that Passes" is a strong statement about the loss of cultural traditions, is it not?

Yes, and that's a very big thing with me.

Portugal figures prominently in Old County Of My Heart. *Why is Portugal important to you?*

The Portuguese have been coming to Newfoundland for five hundred years or more. For me, it goes back to just seeing them on the street all the time, in Newfoundland. They dressed so beautifully, in these gorgeous old wools — very poor, but elegantly dressed. They were fisherman, sailors, and were always very daring. I didn't come into St. John's much, as a young girl, so it was later ... I was working in theatre, and Mary Walsh, from Codco, was doing work at the hall. She was doing a play about the Portuguese in St. John's, and their mixing with the local women. She said she wished she had somebody who would go down onto the boats and invite the fisherman, open up the hall to the fisherman. I said I would go down to the boats, talk to the captains and invite all the ships. I went down to the boats, and had something to eat, and the minute I heard them talking to each other, I fell in love with that language. They played music for me, and that was another thing I fell in love with. Then I had a Portuguese boyfriend. (laughs) My father talked about the Portuguese, too. That's in my poem called "Storm." This Portuguese captain, to my father, was like the hero of Placentia Bay. All that history is important to me, who Newfoundland has been connected with.

I first went to Portugal in '83. I fell in love with it, and started studying the language. I'm almost the only one in Newfoundland who is interested in the Portuguese, although Anita Best and Pamela Morgan are — but there is almost nobody else trying to keep that tie alive. The Portuguese have a musical tradition similar to Newfoundland ballads, Irish ballads.

What other places form your imaginative reference points?

When I was growing up, I heard more about Lisbon and County Wexford and County Waterford, more about Iceland, than Chicago. I also find it a lot more romantically beautiful to be connected with those places than to be connected with Vancouver.

153

And maybe, too, it is because of the language; language has always intrigued me a lot.

There's a part of me that has always felt so removed from Canada; I don't call myself a Canadian. I can't, in all honesty, do it. In some ways, I don't give a good goddamn if they ever recognize us, because I feel more connected to Ireland, to Portugal, Iceland, Puerto Rico, writers from that area. Honest to god, if we all of a sudden drifted off, I'd never miss a single thing.

Your title poem, "In the Old Country of my Heart" suggests a different kind of place, an inner landscape. Can you talk about that inner landscape?

It's probably just that place writers have to go to. For me, it's really connected to my childhood. When I was very young, I didn't have any friends who were readers or writers. I felt like I was really the only person ... I guess every child thinks they're the only person. But I was really aware I was doing something different. My mother used to say "You're going to give yourself bad nerves, from reading." And writing? That was the place that I went to. I think it built that solid core of aloneness.

That inner place, though lonely, seems rich with naming. You've written, "I spoke the world for myself/my secret."

I still do that an awful lot. I love the feel of words.

Do you consider yourself a regional writer?

I think about it more as "place," rather than "region." Maybe it's some of my anger that does that. If things are called "regional," then why isn't this place part of all that regional stuff they're always talking about, up there, you know, in Canada? I don't think about the other "regions." I really only write from this place. I could never think about, say, Portugal, as a "region." It's a place, I love writing about place.

Do you see links between Newfoundland women poets?

In a way, I think women's concerns are pretty universal. It just comes down to how they're expressed. This is where it becomes hard for me to get out of my own small world. Sometimes I've thought maybe it has less to do with where you're from than what class you're from. I think I would find it a lot easier to sit around chatting with a bunch of working class, or poor, rural women from anywhere in the world, than with, say, some merchant's daughter.

Women writers in Newfoundland seem to explore the lives of working-class women quite often, don't they?

It's what you choose to write about — giving voice to what

for so long was not thought of as important. Nobody really wanted to hear about the scrubbing ladies, the cleaning ladies. That side of the coin has, for so long, not been looked at, and finally, there's a voice. That's really important.

There seems to be a pretty close-knit community of writers in St. John's. Can you comment on how that has impacted on you?

I find it a wonderful, interconnected support. There's a sameness in voice that I love. I know what Mary [Dalton] is trying to get at, in her work. I have a close connection to Carmelita [McGrath] geographically because she is from an area nearby to where I was raised. I mean, I know what Margaret Atwood is saying, but I know more of the "underwear" of what Carmelita is saying, if you know what I mean.

Sheree Fitch: The Laundry Hamper and the Moon

"The everyday is sacred. I like to wing to the moon and back, my feet planted deep somewhere, and look at the symbolism of what's underneath my nose. A lot of times, it's the laundry hamper — although these last few years, it could be something as exotic as a cinnamon tree in Zanzibar.

It is the variousness of being in a being that I am fascinated with: even more, whether or not this variousness is connected to something divine outside of ourselves and we are only messengers, mediums, note-takers."

photo: Vaughn Merchant, Cape Breton Post

Sheree Fitch grew up in New Brunswick. She attended St. Thomas University and Acadia University. Her many children's books include Toes in My Nose *(Doubleday 1987),* Sleeping Dragons All Around *(Doubleday 1989),* There were Monkeys in my Kitchen *(Doubleday 1993),* Mable Murple *(Doubleday 1995) and* There's a Mouse in My House *(Doubleday 1997), all of which have won or been shortlisted for awards. Sheree's collection of adult poems,* In This House Are Many Women, *was published by Goose Lane Editions in 1992. She subsequently wrote a play,* Like a Little Candle, *based on that book, which was produced by Eastern Front Theatre in 1996. She travels extensively to read, perform, and educate in schools and universities in Canada and other countries. Currently living in Halifax with her family, Sheree is at work on a second collection of adult poetry.*

Sheree and I conversed by email.

How did growing up in Atlantic Canada impact on your evolution as a writer?

I wanted to become a writer so decided to become a nurse. That pretty well sums up what I thought my chances were of being a writer here or anywhere, for that matter. I didn't finish nursing, but became a mother instead. At seventeen. Here's how I think growing up here affected me most, bottom line: it taught me a lot about living on the edge. It was a place that felt safe, like a nest. It's my home forever, yet it was always a place I longed to escape from. From the time I was seven, I dreamed about the world beyond and knew I would have to travel. Before I could do that in real time, I think writing gave me that sense of departure and exploration and excitement. It was one way to journey to distant lands.

Do you see a "sense of place" in your work, some kind of articulation of Atlantic Canada?

You see very little in what's been published so far. I always seem to dwell in the country that is childhood or with the adult inside a domestic and personal landscape. God knows, it has been most in my face. I really am fascinated with interior realities, the psychological and spiritual worlds of the voices that swivel in my head. It might be that the Land of Old Dish Rags has circumscribed my experience even more than the ocean. But not really.

There is a fierce regionalist in me, though, and I suspect that is showing more in the as-yet-unpublished writing I've been doing these past five years — since trips from the Arctic to Africa to the Himalayas, I am writing about other places and see my Atlantic world in a very different way, as a result.

What people or things helped you emerge as a writer?

Thanks to Nancy Bauer and the Tuesday Night Ice House Gang, Fred Cogswell and the Maritime Writers Workshop, I eventually found some generous, encouraging spirits; this is what made me stay on the planet as well as keep going through ten solid years of rejection before I published.

In the beginning, in New Brunswick, there were no writers of children's work, so I felt a bit weird, you know. I wrote a book called *Toes In My Nose,* after all. But the writers there were enthusiastic and for the most part, I never felt they looked on children's literature as a lesser literature. St. Thomas and Acadia both were communities I needed while studying. The professors there were crucial to my development. In Nova Scotia, the children's literature community is amazing, with people like Noreen Smiley who I met in 1987. Then there was Anne Connor Brimer who said "Keep doing what you do." It was humbling and it made me think I should keep going. I never knew how I would raise two children myself and dare to be a poet!

What about your sense of a literary community within the Atlantic region as a whole?

When I think about the community as a whole in Atlantic Canada, I am excited about what people have done and are doing. Kay Smith and M. Travis Lane — just knowing they were poets and lived where I came from was inspiring. It didn't matter to me if I was writing children's poetry and they were "adult" poets. They were women. They were writers.

The first time I saw Maxine Tynes read, I thought hers was the kind of poetry I liked to read and hoped to write — honest and filled with energy. Carmelita McGrath and Sue Goyette are dazzling poets. Sue MacLeod. There's a poem I read years ago about a woman getting up in the night to do her writing while her house and the world is sleeping. She catches sight of another window with a light on across town and wonders if there is some other dreamer/writer trying to carve worlds out of words in the night. All of us are like that, trying to live and raise our children and love our lovers and somehow write. We are connected by the fact that we try to put pen to paper and pray or lament or rage or meditate with our words. We are connected even if we do not know each other.

You write for both children and adults. How do you negotiate voice? What I mean is, at what point in the writing process are you aware that it's an "adult" voice you're engaging with, or a "children's" voice?

It would be easier if I went *bing*, now I am a child or *bing*, now I am an adult. *Bing*, today I will write a nonsense poem; *bing*, today I will work on a sequence of poems about a man and woman having a slippery love affair, *bing*, now one about an elephant. Sometimes it does get confusing. Even when I am working on a specific project with a deadline, I cheat and then feel guilty for not writing what I am supposed to be writing. I set myself up so long ago to feel guilt and writing together. But money is a factor always. If I have a contract for a children's book or play or whatever, everything else is shoved aside. I have waited for eight years to work on what I'm working on now.

If a word attracts me and I start to play, that will no doubt be a children's poem. That is, unless the word is "condom," for example. I'm not going to write a tongue twister about condominiums and condoms for a children's book. *In This House Are Many Women* includes poems written over a fifteen-year span. The adult ones take longer, are harder on me emotionally to write, but are not necessarily more technically difficult. Writing good nonsense verse is demanding and I still want to do it better and do it until I die. The orality and musicality of language needed to create poetry in works for children is something I still pay a lot of attention to in adult poetry.

Poetry is not a novel meant to be read in silence, and it's not music you'd want to listen to for the duration of a symphony, perhaps. But words out loud in the air moving between people is poetry. When I write for adults I also write for the ears of the reader. Yes, I think of readers although it's not cool to admit it. I hope my adult poetry finds readers; that is the only way a poem comes to life – if it is read not to a wall, not to yourself, to an "other."

What is imagination, for you?

I'm a big Blake disciple and think we cannot talk about the imagination without acknowledging that link to the divine.

Let's talk about your adult poetry book, In This House Are Many Women. *Its title suggests multiplicity. The poems also engage a number of voices and personae — "many women." Why is it important to you to experiment with multiple voices?*

The whole concept of multiplicity of voice or plurality just makes sense to me, a twist on the "many in the one" that goes back to the Romantics. I was also very influenced by Dennis Lee's essay, "Polyphony: Enacting a Meditation," that I came across in graduate school. He wasn't referring to his children's work, but about orchestrating this many "tuned" or multi-toned dimension across the poetic space of an adult work. By voice, too, he meant not just "voice," but an aspect of being. Exploring this allows me to wear the hats or speak in the tongues of others, knowing that at some level, I must search out and connect with some similar voices within myself, uncover or recover those parts of myself. In *In This House,* Lucy and Diana are parts of me, but I am not Lucy or Diana. I am none of the women in *In This House,* but I am all of the women. It is the variousness of being in a being that I am fascinated with, and even more, whether or not this variousness is connected to something divine outside of ourselves and we are only messengers, mediums, notetakers. William Blake talked to angels on a daily basis in his garden. I'm not there yet!

Are there themes your adult writing and your children's writing share?

Certainly, emergence is an ongoing pattern I see in my writing; breaking silence and finding voice — the power of the imagination to do what Blake calls releasing us from the darker world of experience. I wonder if "themes" develop because at any given moment, besides being a writer, you are in the midst of life and the pivotal things you deal with subconsciously find their way into your work. Right now, as my life is in a major transition in terms of my family and motherhood issues (it is always in flux, but sometimes the rapids are the size of Niagara), a lot of my writing is dealing with letting go. Or not being able to. A play I just finished deals with a young girl coming to grips with her father dying. Both my parents were very ill when I was writing that. No coincidence. You write what you need to work out, sometimes. I don't consider this therapy, either; that would be journaling. This is just how life and art intersect. I write and I live, and the crossover that happens between my lived life and my creative life; this can been seen in both the children's poetry and the adult work.

A number of the women in In This House *are marginalized economically or emotionally or spiritually. Some of them have been subjected to domestic violence. These women, some of them, are on the edge; they dream about recovering from the pain, starting over, getting their own place, finding themselves again. A lot of their despair seems symptomatic of patriarchal, capitalist society. Is it important to you, as a poet, to write about social inequities?*

If one writes about what they care about most, and what they care about most is the world and the people in it, then even if we want to say we do not have a social responsibility, we cannot escape it, really. If we care enough to write, we are hoping that what we say makes some sort of difference, even if it's only to one reader.

Your poems are rooted in everyday objects — shampoo, underwear, tampons, shopping malls. Why is this important to you?

The everyday is sacred. We can create our own mythology and must or, as Blake says, we will be enslaved by another man's – including, of course, Blake's, if we're not careful. I like to wing to the moon and back, my feet planted deep somewhere, and look at the symbolism of what's underneath my nose. A lot of times, it's the laundry hamper — although these last few years, it could be something as exotic as a cinnamon tree in Zanzibar. My landscape is changing. Behind any work that stirs me, there is a sense of a human being who has hammered out some philosophy and seen things with a wide-angle lens. There is a difference between art that illustrates a breadth and depth of the human condition and propaganda written to make a statement, or to make me think a certain way. In the adult work, I often write about what terrifies me or disturbs me and the world often does.

The poems in In This House *have a dramatic intensity. Has your work in theatre and broadcasting sharpened your awareness of the poem as a dramatic moment, or was that awareness always there?*

It was my father who taught me that the words *"O wild west wind"* could be dramatic, that poetry was a performance with words. Radio and poetry are a really good match, I think, because of the ear connection and the images being created in the mind of the listener. Poetry had its roots in song and dance and the spoken word, as part of entertainment even, I think radio is a great medium and provides a forum for poets to reach out to a wider audience. They get a few bucks, too. Didn't even Chaucer get paid for entertaining the court, and Shakespeare had to write to keep the crowds coming in? I see nothing wrong with poetry meeting the people and people expecting poetry to entertain as well as "edify" or "enlighten."

In This House *explores the connections between women, perhaps the longing for connections. I'm thinking of poems like "Advice" and "Grand-mere:" "I ache for a woman who swallowed the moon." Are some of your poems a quest for connections, for female mentors?*

Yes. Always. It is also just a reflection of my own life. Without a strong network of women friends and role models, even those ancestors long gone, I would not be here. I believe in that idea of "community" more than organized groups, and always have. In one sense, that is what I saw the shelter [for battered women, in *House*] as a wonderful metaphor for; here are women thrown together who would not normally be friends and in the midst of this crisis time in their lives, they support each other. To me, those poems are about resilience and not about battered women. Anyhow, most of us forge our own communities and need connectedness even when we tend to be extremely solitary as writers. In *In This House Are Many Women*, I hoped I was celebrating women's connections in various communities. I also showed, in some instances, women pitted against each other, as well. It's unflattering, it's ugly, but it's also true.

It must have been difficult to write about physical abuse...? What things motivated you?

I was at a dinner party in 1992. An "educated" woman spoke in such scathing terms about a woman who had left her husband because of abuse that I almost hyperventilated at the dinner table. There was still such a dismissal of someone's life and experience over wine at a dinner party, such intolerance. Mind you, a lot of people sprang to the opposite view that night. I went back to my hotel room that night and tossed and turned and knew I would tell Suzanne [Alexander, Goose Lane Editions] that the shelter sequence needed to go into the book. So I was driven to publish them in one way, and yes, it took courage for a lot of reasons. This was sort of before the wave of books that emerged in the last decade about women's abuse. It seemed risky, at the time. I still find those poems extremely difficult to read.

When the book came out, I walked into a major bookstore chain and was surprised to see it there. They did not have a poetry section. I hoped to see it under women's studies, but where was it? In the psychology section, next to self-help and healing books. Did I laugh? Of course I did!

The women's shelter poems certainly remind us of hazard, what a dangerous place the world can be. Is safety an issue, in your writing?

Right on. My entire life is a quest for a safe place which I know is also illusion. There is only now. I do think there is a universal need or search for this safe place. Some might call it home, but for many, home is not safe, so the notion of "shelter" or safe place suits my understanding better. I know it sounds depressing, but I do believe there are only resting places we get, and these are places within our own psyche, if we can manage. Therapy helps. So does meditation. And walking until you sweat.

In This House Are Many Women *reflects strong feminist concerns. How would you define the feminism in your writing?*

I wrote that work between 1981 and 1992. Many of the poems reflect my own struggle and confusion about what it meant to be a woman questing after her place and identity in our culture at that time. I would say now, almost ten years later, as the mother of two young men, that men have just as many conflicts, that gender has less to do with our struggles than with class/power/money issues. No, I am not reversing my militant feminist position. My feminism has always been inclusive, if for no other reason than I loved my dad and had sons and had to come to grips with not making sweeping generalizations and blaming everything on men. I have always seen oppression as systemic. Any time we fasten too tightly onto any "-ism," we trap ourselves. Labels can be useful but dangerous because of the built-in assumption that comes with them, sticky as velcro. Obviously, you've touched on a subject I like to rant about. As the Buddhist students I taught in Bhutan taught me, often all we can say is, what to do? What to do? And try to do something.

In In This House, *the woman Diana has some of the qualities of a heroine, if a poetry book can be said to have a heroine. Do you want to comment on Diana, the woman who escapes from her stultifying suburban life?*

We all deserve to have some way to fuel our imaginative lives, to create in the midst of our mundane lives because if we don't, we lose our very souls and are reduced to a robotic automatic pilot existence. I wanted to create a character who makes a choice. So Diana is a heroine because she follows her impulse to create and finally chooses to commit to her creating and to her soul wholeheartedly. I created her perhaps for myself as the ongoing commitment to keep writing is not a done deal but a choice I must make over and over and over again. I falter often. I question the worth of what I am doing. I still want to live my life and not just live it wishing I could be writing. Diana, on the other hand, gives herself completely to her art. Diana lives on the moon now, and she is sending down her songs for someone to listen to. That's part of the next book.

What are you doing right now?

Right now, my favourite personal metaphor is that my life is a dot-to-dot puzzle, and I still don't know what picture I am making. I think that is gender-neutral, a "young" metaphor from a game from childhood once again. I'm hoping to have a second adult book ready for the year 2000. I am also writing more directly about "stuff" sacred and spiritual.

Sue MacLeod's Passages and Pilgrimages

"I have a real obsession about place. How do you combine the freedom and mobility we have today with maintaining a sense of what's where and what's what? We want both, we seem to have a *need* for both. People talk about how regionalism or a sense of place is important in literature, and that also makes me think of how important it is in *life*."

photo: Rhonda Knubley

Sue MacLeod grew up in the Maritimes and in Ontario. While still in high school, she began a part-time job as a reporter for a community newspaper, and has worked as a non-fiction writer and editor ever since. In her thirties, she went to Mount Saint Vincent University to take women's studies, and it was there that she discovered poetry. In 1994, she won third prize in the League of Canadian Poets national competition; and her first collection, The Language of Rain, *was published by Roseway in 1995. Recent work has appeared in* Arc, Event *and* The Malahat Review, *and is forthcoming in* Riprap, *an anthology from the Banff Centre Press. Sue has recently completed a collection of linked poems entitled "Mercy Bay." She lives in Halifax with her teenage daughter, Jeanna.*

Sue and I talked in Halifax's Fireside Lounge.

You began writing poetry in your early thirties. Was there a particular trigger that got you started?

I had been working as a journalist for a long time, and when I decided to stop doing that, it opened up the possibility of being another kind of writer. As a kid, I'd dreamed of being a writer — writing stories, writing novels — but for most of my twenties I wrote for money, and for me that didn't fit too well with exploring the other — the imaginative — side. I started at the Mount when I was thirty-two. My daughter was three and I had recently become a single parent, and it seemed like a time to make new choices in my life. I thought I might become an academic because

I wanted to work with ideas and to really be able to delve into subjects in depth. But then, almost immediately, the world of poetry opened up for me. It certainly didn't help with the question of how to make a living (laughter), but it's one of the best things that's ever happened in my life.

Why poetry, do you think?

It's some kind of unconscious connection. Like: this is my language, I understand it and I want to — I *need* to at least *try* — to speak it. In a more political sense, poetry excites me because it celebrates the simple, low-tech power of the individual human voice. In some ways it bridges the gap between oral and literate cultures. It stands there, with one foot in each, and that seems especially interesting now when a third kind of culture is being introduced.

You published an essay called "Talking the Poem" in the journal Event. *In it, you compared writing to having bundles of sticks on your desk. When you rub the sticks together, you spark the poem into existence. Kind of a Promethean moment, I suppose. How do you ignite these "sticks" into poems?*

Picking the right sticks and rubbing them together the right way (laughter). I probably have about a hundred things in my computer by now — things like a first line, a last line, a bit, an idea. I have far more ideas than time, so I have to put these things aside and go back to them when I have a chance. But I find that when I take one of them out to develop it, it won't always work. Something that happens two years from now might eventually click with something I jotted down last week, and *that's* when the poem will be ready to happen.

The other day, I was thinking about something that had to do with hospital workers, and somehow that connected to one of those "sticks" in my computer — some lines I'd jotted down a couple of years ago about *prepositions*, of all things. And I saw a connection between these two totally different ideas, and a poem started taking shape. It's a quirky poem — not surprising, from how I'm describing it — and I kept going back to my desk all day and night and by three in the morning it was pretty well done. That's unusually fast for me, usually it's at least a week or two before I think a poem is ready to show anybody. But that's one great thing about writing: When it's going well, you can wake up and you have no idea what's going to happen that day. It's a thrilling life really — within what might look like a routine domestic existence!

So, many of your poems come into being when two distinct thoughts "rub together" the right way?

Not many of my poems, but a few of my favourite ones have. In *The Language of Rain* there's a poem called "Betrayal," which is about the experience of receiving a Dear John letter. I was trying to write about that, but it seemed too … for lack of a better word, "confessional." Then I remembered a scene I had witnessed on a highway years ago, probably twenty years earlier, that had always stayed with me in a very painful way. I realized that scene — it was a dog chasing a pick-up truck from which he'd been left behind — had the same emotional quality I was trying to express in my poem. By weaving the two situations together, I could get to the poem that I wanted to write.

Which writer or writers have been important mentors to you in terms of learning your craft?

Don Coles is the person I've worked with the closest. That was at Banff in 1993. We must have met about a dozen times, and we went through an earlier version of *The Language of Rain* on a line-by-line basis. I learned so much from him about editing, about making things work and what it means, I guess, to really approach poetry as a professional. A couple of years before that I went to Vancouver, to the Westword Women and Words Workshop. Gay Allison was the facilitator there, and she taught us a lot about poetry — reading it, loving it, celebrating each distinct poetic voice. There was a great deal of reverence for the practice of poetry. Then just this fall, I went to Sage Hill in Saskatchewan and worked with Daphne Marlatt. It was a lifesaver, because I had this linked manuscript — where the poems are all connected, I mean, and not all of them are discrete or self-sufficient — and I really wasn't sure how to work with a linked manuscript. Daphne really helped me to see what was flowing together and what wasn't, and to understand the kind of structure I would need.

You mention Westword, a women's workshop, and Daphne Marlatt, who is known as a feminist writer. Is feminism important in your work?

I don't set out to write overtly feminist poems, but I think everything I write is informed by the way I look at the world, and feminism is part of that. It was in a course on women's writing that I first started writing poetry; we were asked to write something about hands, and I wrote a poem that turned out to be "Bodily Knowledge," and I've been writing poems ever since. That was a long time ago now, and it seems very far away, but I remember the combination of talking about women's writing, and being in the kind of intense and expressive atmosphere of a women's studies program at its best. It was powerful for me and it got me going.

Bronwen Wallace was one of the first poets whose work I loved and admired, and her politics are always present. Not overt, but they're there. They were always there. I think one thing that Bronwen Wallace and other recent women writers have done for poetry is that they've expanded the notion of what kinds of subjects are okay to write about. It's okay now to write about the daily domestic details of life. You don't have go looking for "big subjects," because paying close attention to small moments is enough. If you do that well, there's nothing claustrophobic or self-referential about it.

If you're living a life full of small moments — say, raising small children, for example — the experience of that is bound to pop up in your poetry. And feminism has told us that that's okay, for women and men both. It's okay for a poet or any kind of artist to be creating out of a regular workaday life, muddled up with caring for other people. You don't have to be living a life that is totally free or totally of the mind. And that's a valuable gift that feminism has given us, because it can help to make artists — and art, and creativity — less marginalized in our world.

You belong to a women writers' workshop?

Well, it *was* a women writer's workshop for about three years, but now we also have a man — Brian Bartlett. This writing group is extremely important to me. More important even than the feedback is talking about writing, about our lives as writers, and about poetry we've been reading. The quality of that conversation, and feeling part of something larger, and the reminder that everybody's voice has something unique to add, is important. There's always an atmosphere of respect, and real interest. It takes away some of the sense of isolation that can be a down-side to writing.

How did the poems in The Language of Rain *take shape?*

They were written over a period of about seven years, from the earliest one, "Bodily Knowledge," which I wrote for that class, to the latest one, "Betrayal." There's a strong element of movement from childhood through to the gaining of various types of awareness and experience. The first section deals with passages, as does the whole book really. "What the Dog Dreams" is in that first section, and it's about a family pet, in one sense, but it's also about the passage of a species through time. The rest of the poems in that section are rooted in childhood. Then the second section focuses on romantic relationships; the third section, "Daily Bread," is more political; and the final one, "The Language of Rain" sort of pulls it all together. A lot of the poems in that last section speak from the experience of being a woman, in particular, and that's where the poems about being a mother mostly are. There's more of a sense of resolution in that part.

You use all sorts of material details in your poems — chenille bed-spreads, Pontiacs, Cracker Jacks, fishnet stockings. Why do these details interest you?

I'm interested in particulars. The texture of things. The small details that can pull someone into a poem. Also, some of those things help to place the poem in a historical context.

You mentioned that The Language of Rain *is about passages. You've made pilgrimages too, in your writing and in your life. Can you talk about your recent pilgrimage to Scotland?*

I was there for a writer's retreat, at Hawthornden Castle in Midlothian. I was quite aware of being in an ancestral place be-cause of the Scotland/Cape Breton connection, and both of my parents are from Cape Breton. When I hear Gaelic — and I've made some attempt to learn it, but I haven't yet had the time to focus the way I want — there's a very strong resonance for me. And I think it's connected to rhythm, and rhythm is so much of what poetry is about. I'd like to understand patterns of speech better some day; it seems to me that there is a great deal more music in the way people speak in Scotland than there is here. More of a cadence. And that's really interesting from the perspective of thinking about poetry.

Accents interest me. So much will be lost if we all sound more the same, and it's a process that's already happening. But you can't keep people sounding different because you want them to be quaint and appealing, either. It's a cynical vision, but imagine if the tour-ism department set up schools where people could learn local ac-cents so they could sound good for the tourists. I don't think that's the way to go (laughter). But there's something really sad about a flattening out of how everyone sounds. The BBC are now using people with regional accents to try to avoid that flattening out, so maybe it isn't just poets — who are obsessed with "voice," by nature — who are thinking about these things.

You seem to make a link between "voice" and "place."

Yes, and I have a real obsession about place. How do you combine the freedom and mobility we have today with maintaining a sense of what's where and what's what? We want both, we seem to have a *need* for both. People talk about how regionalism or a sense of place is important in literature, and that also makes me think of how important it is in *life*.

You seemed to be aware of place from very early on. You've mentioned that you only wrote half a dozen poems before your thirties, and the first of these, when you were eight years old, was called "Oromocto at Night."

Funny, that was about twilight, but I perceived it as being about Oromocto, New Brunswick, where we lived at the time.

The Language of Rain *contains quite a few temporary homes — motels, transitory apartments. Why?*

It probably comes from growing up as an army kid, so you don't have a sense that where you're living right now is really home. We'd live somewhere for two years, and then somewhere else, and my mother always spoke of the place she originally came from — Cape Breton — as "home." With army kids of that time, there was often a sense that your parents were from somewhere, but you weren't. Even now, I have a sense of identification with Cape Breton more than anywhere. And that's ironic, I think, because I'm not a Cape Bretoner. It's my parents who were.

That sense of second-hand identity is a reality for many people with Cape Breton roots, I think, and with various kinds of Atlantic roots — people whose families have had to leave here for work. And I imagine there's a similar reality for many second-generation immigrants as well, trying to relate to an "old country," a "home" they've never seen. My particular sense of that second-hand identity is what I've been exploring in the manuscript I've just finished, the linked one, "Mercy Bay."

Is Mercy Bay a real place?

It's a fictionalized place, based on Ingonish where my mother was from.

Let's shift from place to something related, community. Do writing workshops provide a sense of community?

Yes. The Banff workshop really did. This country is so huge, and for a time it seems to shrink.

How do you think your work is evolving?

I think my poems are becoming a little less narrative than they used to be, and that's probably one reason why I'm starting to work on fiction, as well. Because of course I can be more narrative there. The subjects I'm writing about are changing too, of course, but I find there are common threads. I'm also halfway through my third manuscript of poems, which includes the poem "Brick Lane," and right now it's called "A Biography of Rooms." I find it takes the theme of home that's so prominent in "Mercy Bay," and looks at it from new perspectives — how we live in particular places, but how we live in our bodies, too.

Coffee, Anyone? Poetry, Everyone?: Sue Goyette's Everyday Prayers

"The act of writing poetry is as close to prayer as I can get. Poetry is prayer because it sets a light; it magnifies even everyday things. It could be gardening. It could also be making soup for my children. It could be shovelling snow."

Originally from St. Bruno, Quebec, Sue Goyette moved to Nova Scotia ten years ago. She lives with her family in Cole Harbour. Her work has appeared in several literary magazines, including Grain, Malahat Review, Fiddlehead *and* Poetry Canada, *as well as the anthologies* Breathing Fire, Meltwater *and* Vintage '93 and '98. *Sue's first collection of poetry,* The True Names of Birds, *was published in 1998 by Brick Books. It was short-listed for both the pat Lowther and Gerald Lampert awards. She is poetry editor for* Pottersfield Portfolio.

Sue and I talked, over coffee, at Mount Saint Vincent University.

You've been writing for a while, haven't you?

It took me about ten years of exploring my voice before I was confident enough to make it public. As my voice emerged, I gained integrity and tried to challenge that voice with each poem I wrote. You learn to do really creative things with rejections, like origami. (laughs) My first poem was published five years ago in *TickleAce.*

As a poet, what is it you are trying to communicate?

It's a matter of bringing poetry back into the kitchens, making people aware that it's just another way to share the human experience. We do it over coffee. Bronwen Wallace wrote of the everyday kinds of emotional encounters we all face and turned them into art. That's what it's all about. We need to make poetry and the reading of it more relaxed. I'm not saying more accessible; it can still be a challenge to read. But I think poetry is something we can share about things we have in common.

There's a documentary impulse in your writing; you're a close watcher. Have you always been that way?

I kept diaries, which my sister would then use to blackmail me. (laughs) Everyone always watches ... I'm always watching.

Is writing, in some sense, confessional, for you?

Oh, absolutely. I don't think you can hold back, or it's not true. So in that sense, I think it's confessional. It's right on the edge.

Your poems are layered, and dense, and you use quite a long line. Why does the long line appeal to you?

Because of the expansion, the long breath, the unfurling all the way to the end. Longer lines let me explore, all the way to the end. It's a publisher's nightmare; I've had my poems printed, in the tiniest print available, so that they would fit on a line.

How do you create the layers in your poems? When I read your poems, I think, "How did she put this all together?"

There's a space between me and my page, and what fills that space is poetry. When I write, I don't even realize the layers that are being created until the end. I'm incredibly lucky when it happens. And it doesn't happen all the time. Sometimes I have to work at it, and the poems, I think, where I have to work at it are weaker for it.

The way you use domestic objects in your poems is intriguing. You seem to take a lot of inspiration from basic objects around you like vases, rooms, windows, a swimming pool full of rain water. Why is that important to you?

That is incredibly important to me. I write with my desk set up in a hallway, in the middle of bedrooms and windows. And I look at things like crayons and candles while I write. It's something we can all hold and grasp. It's the grounding for my poems. And then, from there, they allow me to go off onto different tangents. But I know I have that stability with those kind of images. I remember when I was five or six, I was watching "The Flintstones." Wilma was hanging this painting up. She wanted to redecorate her house. She got some money and she was wearing a different leopard thing. She was hammering this painting, and it made this big crack in the stone wall. And I remember thinking, "Oh, NO!" (laughs) "What's she going to do?" And she hid the painting and whipped out this little paint can and painted over this crack and made it look like a big painting of flowers, and that it should be there. That stuck with me. I keep thinking, "That's what I've got to do." If all you've got around you is crayons, you take what you can. It's almost like alchemy, and you turn it into something. And that's what stuck with me.

What is the significance of birds, in the title of your new book? Birds appear elsewhere in your work, too.

I love birds. I watch them. *The True Names of Birds* — we put words on things just to be able to communicate the idea of them. But I think a lot of things go beyond that, with words. I think the title and birds, to me, symbolize that "beyond the words." They're so much more that it's impossible just to say "bird," or "bluejay" or whatever, because they contain so much. So when I say "the true names of birds," I think, everything that they really are, and everything that they're not, that we've made them.

On a logistical level, how does a poetry manuscript take shape?

I think it takes a long time to see a bunch of poems as a manuscript. There has to be a unity there. But Erin Mouré said that the first book of poems is usually just a pile of all your good workshop poems. And your second book has to have a plan. I can see that as being true, now. Because my first book is just kind of poems that got published, poems that people liked. And poems that I felt strongly about. Whereas the manuscript I'm working on now has more of a plan. You need to get some kind of anchor in your head so you can go back to that.

You've workshopped at Banff and in Fredericton, but also close to home. Can you talk about the Halifax Poetry Group?

That was a great group. I think James Werner and Brian Bartlett started it. We lasted about four years, I think. We had poets like Carole Langille, Eleonore Schönmaier, Kathy Mac, Lynn Davies, Sue MacLeod, Deirdre Dwyer, Alexandra Thurman. The calibre of writing was astounding. It really made me think about what poems I would bring to the group because the writing was so good. And the feedback was incredible. But groups have a lifespan. Things happened, people got busier. And it kind of stopped for awhile. I'm hoping it'll get started again. I'd get home, feeling total affirmation as a writer.

Is there a sense of a community among women poets in Nova Scotia?

I think there is a community. There are a lot of women poets here. You don't realize until you starting sitting down and listing them, boy. I would think anyone who reads poetry can't deny the power of writing that's coming from women in Atlantic Canada right now.

What impact does place have on you as a poet?

Incredibly, the ocean. When I grew up, we used to go to Cape Cod every summer. I think you can get addicted to the ocean. I'd be in Montreal, after we sold our cottage, and we'd be sitting around in our little apartment, and I'd tell my husband, "I have to see the ocean." So he came here to Cape Breton to work for about a month and fell in love with the place. And as soon as we got work here we just ... we had no family and we knew no one here, but it was really important for us to come here. Within a year, we had that sense of being at home. I love it here. This coast ... it's scraggy and hard. I was driving someone around from Saskatchewan, and he said, "This is the ugliest landscape," and in a way, I can see his point because it's just windy. But I love it for that because it's so alive.

Some of your poems explore relationships between women. I'm thinking of "Sisters" and "Again to Be a Daughter." Why is this important?

Once I had a daughter, it completely changed the way I looked at my mother, for some reason. I think there's an age when every woman and person becomes an adult. I mean, we look at our parents and are no longer the children, but are adults together. We realize the choices our parents had to make, or the way our parents acted, or reacted. All of a sudden you're in the same seat your parents were twenty years ago, or whatever. "Again to be a Daughter" — I wish I had that sense of understanding when I was a teenager, and giving my mother giving complete hell, coming in late, and being really hard to get along with.

A lot of my poems are about women I know. So a lot of people recognize themselves in my poems — girlfriend stories that I kind of made into a poem. That is something that is important to my writing. Girlfriend talk. It's just over coffee

I have this poem called "Women Drinking Tea or Tequila." I think it's true; when women get together, something happens. And within an hour, you're closer to every woman in that room than a lot of people you meet in your life. Most women who I know are so relieved to hear that everyone else has cellulite, that their breasts sag, that there are times when they feel completely inadequate. A lot of women I know are not celebrating who they truly are, which is worth celebrating.

You've also written about motherhood quite a bit. "Motherhood has made me midnight" from "Again to be a Daughter" is a really intriguing metaphor. What does it mean?

That comes from the old Cinderella story, in one way. The ball is over. I was a mother very young. Motherhood is a different headspace, and it made me incredibly aware of my own mortality. I don't think you ever fly, or drive a car, or do anything the same once you have children. And for me, "Motherhood is midnight" means that reality kicks in and you realize you have a child who is completely dependent on you. You're not going to any ball, you're not dressing up. You're getting up at two in the morning and feeding this child. So there's the reality of motherhood.

You occupy an interesting space in this poem, because on the one hand, you live in a world of metaphor. "Motherhood has made me midnight" is a metaphor, and on the other hand, "[T]hings have turned back into what they were" which would imply that the metaphorical layer gets stripped away. So do you occupy a space between the reality, the responsibility of motherhood and the world of metaphor?

I think that's how I occupy my life as a writer. I'm creating metaphors, and then, whether I want to or not, I have to make grilled cheese ... So, you just get this momentum and it seems completely right and true.

Your poems contain striking metaphors. "Regret in all her nightgowns" is only one example. What is the power of the metaphor, for you? And symbols?

They're layered. I live for metaphors. But I would hope that for people who don't read or write poetry that there's something in them that they can take away. I hope they work on a lot of levels. I use poetry to define my life, in a way, and I suppose I look to symbols as a way of putting borders on things. Then I like to break down the borders.

In "This Stone of Knowledge" you write, "[T]here must be a word for this distance." Is poetry writing a search for expression, a search for language?

Absolutely. When you write a poem, in one way, you're trying to box something in, and in another way, let it out. It sounds like a paradox, but, yeah. I was really interested in distance when I wrote that. I was away from home. The English language has a lot of words, but sometimes there isn't one word ... .

You've written, "[R]emember to write down where you plant the tulip bulbs." Is writing a form of ordering for you, or a way of remembering?

It's the cataloguing, the naming. It's a way of saying, "Write me, don't forget me." "Keep me active, keep me a verb." It's like a photograph, a painting of someone. It's a still shot of something that's incredibly important or something that's moved me.

We've talked about birds. Now let's talk about gardening, another motif in your writing. "Each a Different Wish" is one of your gardening poems. The speaker finds a skeleton of a little bird when she's digging. She also contemplates why she gardens. She senses it has something to do with "the absence of wings and being stranded here." Where is "here"?

On the earth, on this planet. Grounded, physically grounded. Contained. In language. The speaker is feeling a lot of grief, and just wanting to be away from all that. And just being at the place where it's kind of becoming a past.

"Each a Different Wish" has a sense of doubleness to it. On the one hand, gardening is creative, but in the poem, it is also a breaking down. Where does this sense of doubleness come from?

I think if you give anything poetic attention it creates almost a doubleness. And that's why poetry, to me, is prayer — because it sets a light, it magnifies even everyday things. I have a poem about a man who rescues a frog. A small simple moment. But that, to me, is prayer. That is saying, "You're just as important as I am and you need to be treated well." So it could be gardening. It could also be making soup for my children. It could be shovelling snow. It's the attention, not necessarily the act. It's what's said, and not said.

You seem to be bringing more and more people into your poems, and the web of connections between them seems increasingly complex. Do you think that you're bringing more of others into your poems?

Yeah, I am doing that consciously because you can only write about your kids getting older so much, and it gets boring for everybody. And it's really important to keep moving. I can write a good, you know, Sharon Olds kind of mother-daughter poem. It's easy. I have to really challenge myself. Because I think it's very easy to get stuck in writing the good workshop poem. I think that's a danger when you're writing: that when you establish your voice, and your rhythm, you can keep repeating yourself. Or you can try to push yourself forward. I think there's a danger of feeling too comfortable. It's important not to recognize your voice once in awhile. Shake it up a bit. And then you can go back and rewrite stuff you're not entirely comfortable with. But I think you have to write on the edge. Otherwise, you're kind of just going in a circle. So my second book is definitely about more people. It also involves faith and prayer. I've realized that writing is prayer.

How is writing prayer? Do you mean that it's a spiritual activity?

I think it's truly spiritual. Not necessarily while I'm writing, but the act of writing. I mean, the act of wanting to record my maple tree dying. It's a way of beholding, I think. It's not religious. I grew up in an incredibly religious atmosphere, but I really don't have much time for conventional religion. When I'm in the act of writing, I think that's pretty well as close as I can get to prayer. Just in the way I'm looking at things, and holding things in my mind.

Heather Pyrcz on Prospect Street

"Prospect Street, where we have lived for the past ten years, is unique in itself. It is in the centre of town, a student street. But it was also the home of others, like Tommy Troke, a friend I admired deeply, who was born, lived, married, raised two sons, and died in the house across from us. I was sitting in my living room, writing, when the black hearse pulled up to her curb. I had never seen death arrive before, and claim its own. I never really understood, until that moment, our mortality. I realized that everything one would ever know is right there in front of us. And I realized this on Prospect Street."

photo: Andrew Steeves

Heather Pyrcz was born in an army camp on the Canadian west coast. Her family lived in various locations throughout Canada, spending seven years in the Yukon. Heather moved to Wolfville, Nova Scotia, with her husband Greg in 1982. They now live on Prospect Street with their children Joshua and Tessa. Heather wrote her MA thesis on Phyllis Webb under the supervision of Donna Smyth at Acadia University. Heather's poems have appeared in a variety of journals and magazines including West Coast Line, Branching Out, The Gaspereau Review, The Fiddlehead, *and* The Antigonish Review. *Heather Pyrcz's first collection of poems is* Town Limits, *published by Gaspereau Press in 1997.*

This interview was conducted over email between Antigonish and Wolfville.

What were your earliest experiences as a writer?

As far back as I can remember, I wrote legends, tall tales. My mother was a librarian and in a number of the places we lived, she had a radio show: *Once Upon a Time* and *Armchair Travelling.* She read everything to us — trying to find effective stories that were 18 minutes long. I wrote imitations. Then, when I was ten, just after we moved to the Yukon, my mom handed me a book. She said we were going to Dawson City, and there was a cabin she wanted me to see — the home of the famous Canadian poet, Robert Service. She said this is a book of his collected poems and that I should read it before we went. We had heard so many intriguing stories of the Klondike. I read all night. And then I started writing poems, and I dropped the other prose forms for a long time. But it was that night, reading the ballads of Robert Service that I decided I wanted to be a poet.

I had a large, dying tree on a cliff overlooking the Yukon River valley that I climbed into to write. I thought I was secretive but everyone in my family knew where I had disappeared to and why.

There is one other incident that deeply influenced my choice of becoming a poet. I was just a little older, maybe twelve. My mother, in fact, was the head librarian for the whole of the Yukon Territory. When we moved to Whitehorse, the library system was housed in a pitiful, wartime house. Well, my mother is a Cape Bretoner, small (four-foot-eleven), but courageous and with vision. She convinced the Yukon Council that Whitehorse needed a cultural centre, and so they built the Whitehorse library. This was in the early sixties. It is still a beautiful building. Besides the library, it also houses two large stone fireplaces, a conference room, a music listening room, and an art gallery. When my mom heard that A.Y. Jackson and his companion Maurice Haycock were painting in the area, she approached them and asked them if they would show their work in the gallery. The method of the Group of Seven was to paint small canvases on site and then take the small canvases home and reproduce them on large canvases in their studios. So Jackson and Haycock showed their field work. They came back a number of times. I remember one showing of A.Y. Jackson's. My parents and brothers had hung the show and it was nearly midnight. My younger sister was asleep on a heap of coats and I was watching the show emerge. It is a fascinating process, like a puzzle picture emerging. I think this is where I learned how art objects can speak for themselves but are also affected by the objects around them. Anyway, the show got hung. Then A.Y. Jackson took my hand. I was terrified. I knew he wanted me to walk around the show with him, to see its effect. For a moment I thought he expected me to give him a critique like I'd seen so many adults give. But after the first painting, he just looked at me and smiled and I nodded, and we moved on. Much later I read a passage from Frost who said, "Let's not be too damned literary — let's just exchange glances if you feel it." This is what A.Y. Jackson wanted that night. I learned something essential — first, that A.Y. Jackson was a kind, gentle man, but also that art has to do with gut feeling.

At university I had important mentors — Sid Stephens, Stephen Scobie, W.O. Mitchell, Donna Smyth.

Phyllis Webb has been an important creative influence, for you. Your long poem, "Night Light," which constitutes the final section of Town Limits, *suggests this. Can you talk about the nature of Webb's influence on you?*

Webb's influence is pervasive. She taught me to think of poetry as a dialogue with the past, present, future, but the writer I most often find myself responding to is Webb herself. She writes in *Hanging Fire* — the proper response to a poem is another poem. Some poets engage you. She gives poets so much to think about, to respond to, both in the way of content and form. She taught me about the line, the breath, intertextuality — the way texts are related to and dependent upon other texts, paradox, and the polyvalent nature of language. This was exciting stuff. Along with Donna Smyth, Phyllis' critical and creative writing is deeply lodged in my imagination.

Along with Webb, Rilke seems an important influence on you. Why do Rilke's "terrible angels" appear in your poetry?

Rilke is one of the beloveds that I keep beside my bed. "Duino Elegies" is one of the frequented rooms of my imagination. Rilke's angels are a reminder — *mortis memento* — remember death. Rilke says we call on them, serenade them, yet, "if the dangerous archangel took one step now/down towards us ... it would kill us." They represent many things — our greater existence. They remind me that what we do as writers is dangerous — that it is no game to explore what we don't yet know or understand.

Town Limits *begins with the two-stanza lyric, "Cup of Coffee." In it, you compare poetry and coffee: "Poetry, like a cup of coffee, / is a dark mystery contained, / framed by the familiar form." Doesn't this capture the essence of many of your poems?*

"Cup of Coffee" is a distillation of my poetics. Poetry, for me, is the expression of the mystery of our everyday existence. The form frames in two ways — contains it, makes it possible — as vessel — and betrays that attempt. "Cup of Coffee" expresses the paradox of writing.

What message does the title of the book send to the reader?

I was hoping that the title would signal that this book is about community — small-scale democracy — the poetic possibilities of everyday life. It also acknowledges our limitations. But there is both the idea of boundaries, outer limits and the way small-town life constrains us. "Nowlan's Canteen" was meant to express the opposing drives within small town life: to stay and to leave.

There is also much of the Annapolis Valley in your writing: Blomidon, tidal bores, the basin. Your metaphors sometimes articulate a Maritime space — comparing truth, for example, to something "slippery/as algaed rocks." How is place important to you?

When I first left the North, I missed the mountains, but now the "sea is all about us." I think we write out of the physical, the body and the landscape. Annie Dillard is another writer I respond to — my journal is full of notes to her. For me, her work exemplifies how what we know is connected to our ability to see the world around us. To see ourselves in the dyke, the orchards, a grain of sand. She constantly reminds me to look at my world. She can find us in the antics of the smallest inchworm and the remotest of continents.

Do you call yourself a "regional writer?"

The expression startles me. It is also ironic because for years I thought I'd never be accepted because I didn't have roots, a region to call my own. One of the reasons I took to Webb was because she evaded those kinds of labels — "regional," "Canadian." She says she fears anyone who is so defined because labels are boundaries that limit us. She says "It is a question of relative values." We have to transcend those boundaries. We write out of our lives, the landscape, out of what we feel, we see, but our writing relates to the larger vision — a human image on an M-type planet.

Interesting, given how localized much of your writing is. Why is Prospect Street in Wolfville important to you as a poet?

After many years of moving around the country, Wolfville is where I finally put down roots. That is a remarkable experience. For the first time in my life, I stayed somewhere long enough to watch children grow up, to see change occur before my eyes. My life has always been transient, mutable, moving.

But Prospect Street, where we have lived for the past ten years, is unique in itself. It is in the centre of town, a student street.

Greg and I have lived our life together in communities of students — I count myself fortunate in this. But it was also the home of others, like Tommy Troke, a friend I admired deeply, who was born, lived, married, raised two sons, and died in the house across from us. I was sitting in my living room, writing, when the black hearse pulled up to her curb. I had never seen death arrive before, and claim its own. I never really understood, until that moment, our mortality. I realized that everything one would ever know is right there in front of us. And I realized this on Prospect Street.

What is the poetic process, for you?

The poetic process is a constant movement like the tides. It is in the ebb and flow of the inner and outward life that we keep the balance — seeking the articulation of intuitive understanding, found within, of those objects, ideas, emotions that are outside us. Life is one half of the metaphor; that whatever we see is a vehicle to understanding something beyond us. And that's what we are after, greater understanding.

The third main section of Town Limits *concerns itself, to some extent, with questions of language, "the problem with abstractions," problems around naming, precision. Is there a way in which language itself "limits" you?*

Language does have serious limits for me. But perhaps it's not so much language as the taboos that govern language, speech. Bergman said, in "The Rehearsal" — if I took off the mask and said what I feel, you'd turn on me in fury. It is so hard to call things by their proper names — so many taboos, the unspoken, the failure of words to express what you feel, the terror in the recognition of what you are about to say, the anguish words can evoke, especially words of truth. And so we entertain, distance the stark truth with metaphor, analogy, allegory, humour, irony, layering the meaning so it comes to us gradually in a form we can accommodate.

Town Limits *is a brave book. I mean, here you are, living in a university town and writing about it in a recognizable way. Has this caused you any anxiety?*

There is a certain degree of terror when you are trying to get it right. When "it" is other people's lives, experience. People that you know and face every day. Knowing that you and they will still be here tomorrow. There is a line where you can overstep their privacy. I don't want to cross that line. But at the same time I am bearing witness; I don't want to back away from those images that reveal our humanity. I keep hoping that if I get it right, I will just be thought of as "poet." There is a kind of self-imposed isolation in that. Kafka called it "a freezing solitude."

There's a remarkable range of emotional tonality in your poems. This includes anger, which has sometimes been a taboo emotion for women. Obviously, that taboo is connected to a stereotype about women. How important is it to you to give voice to anger?

I have no trouble expressing it. I want to express all our emotions, just as I want to be able to look at the whole of life. The poems come; what is difficult is leaving them in the collection or sending them out — knowing they jangle, irritate, annoy. But yes, to tell the truth, I think they are necessary. Martha Nussbaum is a philosopher I admire. In her work she explores Aristotelian anger — she later refers to "poetic justice" — but she is concerned with measured anger, anger aimed at the proper objects. Aristotle calls emotions, like anger, guides to ethical truth. I don't think, therefore, that we can afford to jettison emotions like anger.

You've written in "Motherlode," that "I wanted to be the perfect mother." To what extent is your identity as a mother in conflict with your identity as a poet?

I try to keep my life in balance — mother, wife, teacher, poet — and not to cheat any one of these identities. The conflict comes between the ideal and the real — motherlode/motherload — what Doris Lessing refers to as the gap between what we aspire to and what we do, rather than conflict between the roles.

You've written about aging and menopause in poems like "44" and "menopausal storms." Why is it important to you to bring the rhythms of your own body into your poems?

I started in dance. I agree with Pound that we lose something essential to poetry if we get too far away from music, and that rhythm is the most primal of all things known to us. The rhythms of our bodies are the rhythms of our lives, and they echo and reverberate in so many of earth's rhythms. Rhythm is how we are connected to the whole. And how we feel that connection. It's another of the functions of the poet, to remember the languages of earth and body. I fear a loss of these languages as we become more and more virtual.

In "Tai Chi," you've written "Attend to the breath." Certainly, that is important in the Eastern arts. How is it important in poetry?

The breath is part of the language of rhythms. Pound, Charles Olson, and Webb all talk about the length of the line, and how it is dependent on the breath. How psyche means breath. There is a connection, then, between line, breath, psyche; Olson says line, breath, heart. Attending to the breath in Tai Chi, as in poetry, puts you in balance, in tune not only with yourself, but with the universe, the music of the spheres.

"Generations" in Town Limits *concludes with "A Chorus of Old Women" who plead "[P]lease,/won't someone/find us a new/country" What would this new, and, presumably, better, country look like?*

The discontent has to do with the failure of the imagination. Timothy Findley argues for the central role of imagination in our lives. He argues that before we can realize it, we must imagine it. I just don't think that we have mapped the entire geography of the heart or mind. I am dreaming of a country of equality, of a love that is all encompassing.

"Night Light," the final poem in Town Limits, *interweaves domestic detail and the image of the spiral galaxy, the Yeatsian gyre. The poem's speaker says it's "time/to leave purgatory for paradise. There must be a way. Straight ahead." Yet later in the poem the speaker calls herself a "lost signal." Is "Night Light" a poem about losing yourself or finding yourself?*

She is a lost signal only when she looks back, like Lot's wife. History makes her a lost signal. "Night Light" is about imagining what Donna Smyth calls a new mythos; it's about looking forward into the dark.

Is "rejecting history," or, at least contemplating that possibility, part of reaching for that new mythos? The speaker of "Night Light" contemplates "rejecting history." What would it mean to "reject" history?

History/herstory. In "Night Light" I'm rejecting someone else's story of who I was/am. All of us who have been marginalized, whose story wasn't fully told, or told falsely, must reject those stories and rewrite our own, no matter how difficult.

In "Night Light," you describe your "terrain:" "This is my terrain: family, myth, spacetime, late night work." This is a complex terrain. How do all these things come together for you, or do they?

Yes. I think most of us have lived inside myths — particularly family myths which can be destructive. Women have also lived inside destructive social, patriarchal myths. I think part of what I want to explore is the difference between destructive and creative myths. In "Night Light," myth becomes equated, for me, with art. So family, art, their space/time are all illuminated for me in late night work which encompasses laundry & writing — it is the space/time that working mothers get to think, reflect, create.

Do you have a strong sense of being part of a community of writers in Atlantic Canada?

No. But my lack of community is my own fault. I am not a joiner. I am, in many ways, a recluse. But that is beginning to change. I've just taken on greater activity in the League of Canadian Poets so I will have to find my community of poets here in Atlantic Canada. Actually, since I've joined the League, I'm beginning to be connected to poets not only in the region but in the country. I can't describe the elation, sitting in the Mocambo Café in Victoria, BC last year, in a room full of poets. It certainly thaws that "freezing solitude."

What are your greatest challenges, as a writer? As a poet in Atlantic Canada?

I think my biggest obstacle is the fact that I'm a late bloomer. That, and the fact that I don't send much out. I have a terrible block when it comes to submissions. And a single rejection can shelve a poem. We also have to deal with the fact that there is no money in writing poetry. Most of us have to find day jobs which restrict the amount of time one can write. I also chose to have a family, and therefore to divide my time further. I don't think of teaching or family life as obstacles — it's just that I chose a route that was going to slow down any vocation. It turns out that it is the pace I'm best suited for.

As a poet in Atlantic Canada? I think the challenge is the same everywhere and that is to tell the truth. To try to see beyond repression, prejudice, ideological limitations. To bear witness to our time and place. But also, to go forward into the dark, to imagine a new mythos, to find a new field where we can create.

Lynn Davies, Traveller

"Geography is really important to me. In Newcastle, our house bordered on a lot of fields and forest. This 'otherness' was always there. I love it there, but I could write other places; I like to be flexible, and I like to leave for awhile, too. But this is the place I love the best."

photo: John McConnell

Lynn Davies was born in Moncton in 1954. She grew up in Newcastle and Moncton. Lynn studied journalism and English at Dalhousie University. After graduating, she travelled extensively. Lynn and her family now live in Fredericton. Lynn's poems have appeared in numerous journals including The Fiddlehead, TickleAce, Contemporary Verse II, Grain, Zygote, *and* The Windhorse Reader: Choice Poems of '93. *Her poem "The Flamingo" won the Lina Chartrand Poetry award from* Contemporary Verse *in 1995. Lynn's first collection,* The Bridge that Carries the Road, *is forthcoming from Brick Books in 1999.*

Lynn and I talked in a café in Fredericton.

You are a much-travelled poet. Of all the places you have travelled, which ones made the greatest mark on your imagination?

Newcastle. There was so much outdoors there. And when I was travelling, I spent a summer in northern Norway, working on a farm. I was isolated because of language, and it was a very isolated community. They spoke nothing but Norwegian. That really made a difference in how I looked at things. To go back and look at my journals now, from that time period ... just the amount of detail I was becoming interested in.

Have you always kept journals?

Always. Ever since I was a teenager. I never thought of audience, and I would have died if anyone had found them!

How did you get into writing poetry?

When I left school, I was travelling around and freelancing for magazines and newspapers. Eventually, I registered in journalism at King's College, but I ended up taking English, which was just great, because it exposed me to all kinds of writers I wouldn't have gone looking for on my own. When I finished school, I continued to freelance, but then I got interested in other forms of writing. Writing for kids. John had gone back to school for his Ph.D., and we had two little kids. I couldn't continue writing the longer forms I had gotten interested in, so I began to write poetry. This was about 1988. Poetry seemed to suit me, the little pieces of time I had, my temperament. I've been hooked ever since. When I began to start writing poetry, I went back to Patrick Lane. When we lived in Prince George, he had come to read one time, and I'll never forget that reading. You read him, and then of course you read Lorna Crozier. I like humour, and she can do it. I was going back to some of the poets I had liked in university — George Herbert, Chaucer, because of the detail and the storytelling. Dante. Going to workshops like the one at UNB gave me more exposure to Canadian writers.

Where do your poems come from? They sometimes depict funny situations, like meeting a cowboy on the Newfoundland ferry.

Some poems are really taken from my life. Alden Nowlan talked about doing "verbal transcriptions." He writes down what other people say, and that's it. Sometimes that happens; the poem is there, and what's happened is enough. Other times, of course, you begin to play around with it and turn it into something else. But yes, that one ["My Silent Days"] is based on personal history.

Your poems draw on vernacular language a lot, and popular culture. Has that been an aspect of your style since you started writing poetry? Can you talk about how your writing has evolved?

Some of those early poems are more stylized, more consciously employing certain rhythms and stylized language, and metaphors. I think I began to relax with language, after a while. I think having children is part of it; it just forces you to relax with a lot of things. Even everyday stories from newspapers can give you poems, the language in them. That's why I admire someone like Alden Nowlan; his poems almost sound like they're spoken casually.

Do you think women poets exploit vernacular speech patterns to the same extent?

Sue MacLeod does, I think. And Bronwen Wallace; her language sounds very casual.

*Some of your poems suggest hazard, the dangerous in the everyday –
I'm thinking of "Tonight the Violent Wind." But they also suggest something
transcendent in everyday life. Is it important to you, as a writer, to be
able to confront both?*

Yes! Writing is a kind of seeing, and I'm not interested in se-
lective seeing. I want to see it all; I'm greedy. "Tonight the Vio-
lent Wind" came from a newspaper story, from something that
actually happened close to Dartmouth. All the little domestic things
that go on in my everyday life are a really important source of
material for me.

Music seems to be an important source for you, too...?

I love music, especially instrumental music, and also, when
I'm writing, it's really important what the poems sound like —
what they sound like out loud, the sound of the words. Some-
times I wish I could write the way certain pieces of music sound.
Music can jolt my thinking sometimes. Sound without words —
it's amazing, yet so expressive. Music creates different voices, and
I love experimenting with voice. I love old music, classical music,
and I really like country music.

What is it about country music that appeals to you?

(laughs) Oh, it's all like one big metaphor for life. It's sort of
cornily vernacular. And funny. One of my poems was based on a
country singer. I got the story from the newspaper, and used a lot
of details from that; then often the story takes off on its own. This
singer had such a bad luck story, getting his records made.

*Your poems are playful, often humorous. Sometimes, the humour seems
to involve someone's ego being undercut. Is that the case in "Briefly, Abelard
Tries to Understand?"*

It does seem to me that the female in the poem is comment-
ing on something about him, maybe his over-inflated work ethic,
or his hunting ethic. She is trying to show him that there's an-
other way of seeing the world.

Childlike perspectives seem important in your work, too...?

I think having children really helped open my eyes to a lot of
things. I stayed home with them, spent a lot of time with them.
You begin to see the world the way they're beginning to see it.
I've written a lot about my kids; sometimes the poems work, some-
times they don't.

*How do you write your poems? Some seem close to prose. Is form
something you are conscious of experimenting with?*

I never really think of it as experimenting. Some poems just seem to come as a little chunk of prose. I always get suspicious when they get too long; they seem to be evolving into something else. Some poems just seem to come that way. I've tried rewriting them, but some of them just insist on being written that way.

You have a very visual sensibility, and you use a lot of fire imagery in your poems. Do you want to comment on that?

I love fire. Paintings of fire (often at dusk) by Mary Pratt just fascinate me. I also like images of vivid colour against a dark background. I'm attracted to that in other people's writing, too. I was reading Seamus Heaney. One of his images was of the Russian writer, Pasternak, sitting in his study at dusk by the fire. That bit of vivid colour in all that dusk and darkness.

There's a lot of motion, in your work, cars, and travel. Why does this appeal to you?

I love to travel. I think it's also a technology thing. I'm really interested in how we relate to all this technology in our lives. The poem in Julie Bruck's book about the car siren and how it is programmed to talk back to anybody who comes close to it, is really funny, a quirky observation of how technology is present in our lives. The last image is of a woman coming out of a bank, and she is really startled because she has heard the voice of a past lover coming out of the car. It really interests me.

What about readings? Have you given them? If so, what value do they have for you?

It's the business of the audience. It's a kind of generosity, in a way. You get a chance to spend yourself, and to ignite little fires in other people's heads. But I'm not a performer; the voice, for me, matters so much. I tend to get very nervous, for readings, and the nervousness will affect my voice often. But it's still a way of being heard. It's a little like learning how to swim; I learned to swim in my late twenties. Once you relax in deep water, you realize that what you were afraid of is incredibly buoyant. I think it's the same with audience, there is a wonderful buoyancy. It gives additional life to your work, to your words. It's a way to keep the words alive — that's what a reading is.

What value have workshops had for you?

The other writers you meet. I met Jan Zwicky here [in Fredericton], and she has been a mentor for me, over the years.

You need to know when a poem is not working for other people. I mean, you have a lot of inside information about a poem; the reader doesn't always know that. It's been pointed out to me sometimes that the reader needs to know more. I always like what Mary Oliver said: Think about a poem as travel in a foreign country. It has to become self-sufficient, so it can survive on its own in a foreign country. I often think of that.

You're in transition, having just moved to Fredericton. Who is your community of writers now?

I'm still in close touch with people I've left behind in Halifax. I'm still in touch with some of the people from Banff. There are different kinds of communities, aren't there? — the localized community, and the larger community. They're all valuable. Email makes it possible, too, to be part of a larger community. I keep in contact with some writers I would lose contact with if not for email.

Can you talk about how place is important to you as a poet?

Geography is really important to me. When I was at Banff for five weeks, towards the end of that time I began writing new work. Those mountains were creeping into the poems. It's such a different geography. I think I would react to any kind of geography I live in. But the Bay of Fundy ... I used to camp beside it and walk beside it and play beside it ... that seems to be important to me. And there's also a kind of restlessness to the Bay of Fundy that I just love! — the way it goes way, way out and exposes its different landscapes, and then comes way, way back in and does that over and over again. In Newcastle, our house bordered on a lot of fields and forest. I remember being outside a lot, by the river, in the forest. I remember seeing forest fires burn from our front living room window. This "otherness" was always there. I love it here, but I could write other places; I like to be flexible, and I like to leave for awhile, too. We were in Vancouver, and Boston, for a year. But this is the place I love the best. I'm so glad we stayed in the Maritimes; it's where I grew up, particularly around the Bay of Fundy. It just makes me want to write. It makes me want to say something.

Shari Andrews, Poet of New Denmark, N.B.

"My writing is more and more tied to landscape. Even though the New Denmark area is very well settled now, and cultivated, there's still a roughness, country roads that wind through the hills. I wanted to tell the story of this place, its history."

photo: George Andrews

Shari Andrews' poems have appeared in numerous publications such as Canadian Literature, Event, The Antigonish Review, The Fiddlehead, Grain, The New Quarterly, *and* Pottersfield Portfolio. *Her chapbook,* Treason, *was published in 1990 by Wild East. Shari's first full-length collection is entitled* The Stone Cloak *(Oberon, 1999). Her manuscript,* Bones About to Bloom, *received the Alfred G. Bailey prize in the 1997 Writers' Federation of New Brunswick competition. Shari is a member of the Wolf Tree Writers group and a contributing editor to* The New Brunswick Reader. *She lives in New Maryland, New Brunswick.*

I talked with Shari in Fredericton.

What writers impressed you, as a child?

Lucy Maud Montgomery. I really identified with Anne's love of words, and the vivid imagery in the books. I had a romantic notion about being a writer. There was one room upstairs in our house that wasn't finished. It had an old table or desk. I would go in there and imagine that I was a writer. (laughs)

When did you begin writing seriously?

After the 1987 Maritime Writers Workshop. I had been planning to do it for a number of years. When my children were still young, I didn't have the time to write very often. During the workshop, a total change took place in my writing. Richard Lemm was our main instructor. After the workshop, Roger Moore, a teacher at St. Thomas University, agreed to work with me. In December, 1987, I got my first acceptance from *Poetry Toronto,* edited by Maria Jacobs.

So you "found your voice" as a writer in 1987?

You're always refining your so-called voice. But identifying yourself as a writer is a major step in the process of finding your voice. For me, voice depends on subject matter, quite often. The majority of poems in my work on New Denmark are narrative and fairly accessible. This form seemed natural to me because I wanted to tell the story of this place, its history. However, both before and since completing this work, I have written poems that are surreal and dreamlike. These two styles are quite different, yet similarities can be seen in the kinds of images and metaphors I use.

Some of your metaphors seem almost scientific. In "Relics" [in Treason*], for example, you use a telescope to suggest poetic vision. Why?*

It has to do with looking at something very carefully. In other poems, I've used petri dishes, things like that.

You also use images of mapping, measuring. In "The Sewing Room," there's an almost scientific quality to the grandmother's sewing because it is so much like mapping. What the speaker's grandmother is mapping, the poem tells us, is "a graph between logic and emotion." Is that what poetry is, for you?

In some instances, poetry is a way of making emotions concrete. It might be on a graph, or described as a visual picture.

How does place, whether it is a room from your childhood, or a field in New Denmark, impact on you?

My writing is more and more tied to landscape. It definitely impacts on my creativity. We lived in Moncton for a number of years. I remember telling a friend, "If we ever get back to Fredericton, I really think I'll be able to write again." We enjoyed Moncton, but it just didn't give me the same richness, the kind of spirituality I feel within the visual landscape around Fredericton.

Why is New Denmark important to you?

My grandmother is Danish. Her great-grandparents came over in 1876. A lot of my childhood memories came from New Denmark. We spent a great deal of time visiting in New Denmark. I spent a great deal of time outside, too, as a child. The contrast struck me between New Denmark, which is rural, and Fredericton, which is more developed. To go to New Denmark was exotic, for me.

How did the pioneering era in New Denmark spark your imagination?

After *Treason,* I went through a period of flux. The poems that started coming out were from my childhood memories. Quite often, they were about New Denmark. There was a definite landscape there; I decided to focus on that. I received a Creation grant from the province. For me, it became a vivid story. I did a lot of research at the archives, and interviews with longtime residents of New Denmark. Having a personal connection to the community had a tremendous impact on the actual writing. Even though the area is very well settled now, and cultivated, there's a roughness, country roads that wind through the hills. I could see how difficult it must have been, and I could relate to it, in some respects.

Was immersing yourself in this landscape a way of reclaiming an ancestral past?

I think it is. If a poem has been triggered by memory, then it's almost like filling in a puzzle, to make what is actually going on clearer and clearer. Often, I'll get a visual image that is foggy. It's like looking at it carefully and filling in the details. There's a message for me in it. That's what writing a poem does; it clarifies things for me.

As well as landscapes, you write about physicality, bodily experiences. This is especially evident in your earlier poems. You've written about the body as a spoiling crop, the body spilling the way kerosene does. Why has "writing the body" been important to you?

Writing that somehow enabled me to write the New Denmark poems. Emotions were closely tied to an actual physical experience. I think I'm still "writing the body," in the recent poems. The body is like life. We like to think we have control, but we often don't. It's almost a metaphor for that.

You've described writing as "leap[ing] up now/to speak of anxious things." There's a sense of anxiety, even trauma, in your earlier work. Is writing a way to speak of anxious things?

It is, in many ways. But there's also something shining: "From this place bring something shining/absolute proof, and you will be safe" ["Myths from my Childhood"]. That "something shining" could be memory, a kind of confidence, a good thing.

There does seem to be more affirmation in your recent work. In "The River Back With Us," you write: "[W]e/brought the river back with us, slipped cool skin between/the sheets and swam." What is going on here?

Because of these physical sensations, a new awareness has come about. An awareness that we are connected physically and spiritually to the natural world.

193

"The River Back With Us" suggests that we carry landscapes inside us, that we internalize them...?

We do, through memory.

You have a strong community of writers in Fredericton. What about writers in the rest of Atlantic Canada?

I have met other writers from the region at the Maritime Writers Workshop, but other than that, no.

So the community is quite localized, for you?

Yes.

Can you talk about your involvement with the Wolf Tree Writers?

There's a real support in the group. We often write together. We've been meeting for three or four years at each other's homes, once a month. Our writing speaks to each other's; it's another level of communication. To prepare for a performance, we'll all bring work. Somebody will start off, reading. Often, that will trigger a paragraph or even a complete poem somebody else has that fits, maybe through its imagery. We fit the performance together that way. We thought we should share what we're doing with the community.

What's a wolf tree?

It's an actual term. It's a forestry term for a type of tree that grows by itself in a grove of other trees. It can get quite large, and sort of misshapen, the branches twisty. It's seen as a tree that is not very valuable because of its shape. But in reality, it provides a home for birds and other wildlife. It's a nurturing tree. We were trying to think of a name for the group. Several of us use animal and nature imagery. We thought the wolf tree was sort of a neat analogy for what we do as writers.

Restless Anne Simpson

"You are always on the outside as a writer. You are never within the culture. And so it doesn't surprise me being on the edges of a culture, which is where I am."

photo: Donald Lee, The Banff Centre

Anne Simpson is an artist and writer who lives in Antigonish. Her poems have been published in various journals across Canada. In 1998, she received Honourable Mention for the League of Canadian Poets Chapbook Competition, and won second prize in the Arc Poem of the Year Contest. In 1997, she was one of two winners of the Journey Prize for her story "Dreaming Snow," first published in The Fiddlehead. *Anne is currently at work on a poetry manuscript, a novel and a children's book.*

I talked with Anne at my dining room table in Antigonish.

How do you think being a visual artist influences your writing?

I must see things before I write them. If I'm writing about banal things like golf courses or suburbia, I have to see them clearly. I get at the intellectual properties of the poem by going to sensual aspects of it, and then working through the ideas.

Can you talk about the transition from visual art to writing?

Writing was always kind of secondary because I thought I would be doing art. It's almost as though when I am not painting, or making a collage, I put it into the writing. I find that in writing I don't have the same angst as I used to. There was always this division between representational and abstract art. Once I started really writing more, I didn't find any divisions. I could always play with writing. I switched from being an artist to a poet to a fiction writer because it allows me to do different things. I get bored if I am doing the same thing all the time. I have to move around a lot.

Can you identify some things that pulled you into writing?

In university I got really got interested in it and I started going to a writing group at Bronwen Wallace's house in Kingston. We would bring our poems and we'd talk. Bronwen was so generous; she would say, "Have you read this, have you read that?" or "I think you need to read this." She was so full of life. She would read her own work, from time to time, and it was really very interesting. I didn't know then just how good she was.

What intrigues you about poetry?

I'm learning that you can resist all the boundaries. I was reading Erin Mouré recently and was intrigued by the plasticity of the writing, the playfulness, the interest in experimenting with things. It's the restlessness in me.

It's not unusual for you to use Ontario landscapes in your poems. And given the importance, to you, of seeing things, how do you write about Ontario now that you've relocated to Nova Scotia?

Sometimes that can be a problem. I was always taking notes when I was in Ontario for the summer, in Burlington, the place where I grew up. And I remember a short-story writer saying once that you should write down everything. If you leave a place of inspiration for a poem, or a series of poems, it's really quite hard to get all the sensual details back in.

Your writing can be pretty edgy, dark. It focuses a lot on violence and disaster. There is an undercurrent of catastrophe. Why do these things interest you?

I'm probably better at writing that kind of stuff. I'm not very good at writing the day-to-day things. I think that's why I had trouble with journal writing, because I got tired of "This is the weather today, and the snow is coming down again." (laughs) I'm not good at the ordinary.

I'm interested in violence. Annie Dillard, in *The Pilgrim at Tinker Creek*, talks about violence and beauty. I'm compelled by that. Take something very sensual and beautiful, like the golf course in Burlington. To me, the thing that is interesting about this kind of landscape is when you show the aspects of violence that are a part of it. This is not the kind of tranquil, peaceful thing it purports to be. There's something here that is wrong with the world at large. I am very hard on suburbia. When I was writing about the golf course, what occurred to me was how we're ruining this world.

What do you mean?

I see an absolutely beautiful landscape with velvety green grass, but just beyond it, the bay is badly polluted. Across the bay are the steel factories. I saw this as a sort of image for writing about the world at the end of the twentieth century. I wanted to write a series of poems about something larger — not just a personal poem — that has to do with our century and what is wrong with it.

Your poetry manuscript is entitled The Floating Museum. *How did you get interested in the museum as a poetic concept?*

Here are all these things *housed* in a place. Often, when you look at the museum as a whole, like the Royal Ontario Museum, you could look at it as higgeldy-piggeldy, except that someone put these things all together, so they see it as connected. I started doing this, started seeing everything as a museum. Our minds are museums, the way we retain and hold onto things, memories. They may be connected. Even the domestic museum: somebody's house. I am fascinated by people's houses because they *house* things. I'm fascinated by the holding of things, the containing of things, and the fact that you cannot hold onto things, you can't contain things. Everything is transient.

Like the butterflies pinned in glass cases you've described?

We are reminded of how they were when they were animated, when they had life, when they were real. Any time you walk into a museum there is this paradox between death and life. It's poignant when you see these beautiful things, like butterflies, and then they are pinned in cases. The whole thing with museums is that they have to do with memory.

Why is the museum "floating"?

I'm very aware of the multiplicity of things. There are always different ways of looking at the world. I think it's the feeling of not wanting to be trapped.

What kind of poetry do you want to write?

I am afraid of the "pretty line" because I am so apt to do that. I don't want to write pretty poems, and I think the harsher stuff offsets this, you know? I'm so in love with the lyric, but I resist it.

How do you think moving to Nova Scotia has impacted on your writing?

I'm not sure to what extent it has had an effect on my poetry. But it has had a significant effect on my fiction. It has allowed me to have a different voice than I ever expected. Place definitely has an effect; you start to write by looking around you. There's a whole culture here that has had an effect on me: the close community, the slow pace, the landscape of rolling hills, ocean, gray clouds, weather. The voice that I have found myself taking on may be very similar to what I may have had if I were in Vancouver, or

Toronto. But I have a feeling it has something to do with this place; it's a very real, very authentic place. I think your voice adjusts to the place that you are in. I'm a "come from away," so I don't resonate with all the same influences that somebody who has lived here for all her life would have. But that might not be a bad thing — you can observe from a distance. You are always on the outside as a writer. You are never within the culture. And so it doesn't surprise me being on the edges of a culture, which is where I am. That gives a sort of strength to my writing, though in some ways, it is very hard for me to be on the outside. But I think that *lack* has propelled me to write, to go where I never would have gone.

You've written a poem sequence called "Postcards from the Outdoor Museum." What attracted you to the "postcard?"

It started with a visual kind of "hook" — in this case it was photographs of the killing fields in Rwanda. One was a photograph of a man standing beside some skulls, and they were just piled up like eggs. What they decided to do was leave the bodies there, and the skulls in an outdoor hut. They are doing this because they want people to be reminded. This is an outdoor museum; it's to remind people, wake people up. This is the way the bodies looked when they fell, for instance, you see a woman's foot, bits of cloth, fragments of bodies. That's why I have to talk about something that's larger than myself. Poets are the ones who can look at it closely, make people cry about it. I'm not saying that I have that power but we do have a responsibility as poets to bring things to the attention of others.

What do you need to write?

I need a lot of space in which I'm not writing. I need a lot of time to dream, and just think, take in, absorb. And then I need a lot of time to write, though I work very efficiently, very fast.

Sometimes you write poems, sometimes fiction, sometimes children's fiction. Why do you like to move around genres?

It's restlessness, as opposed to anything else. I often feel constrained by boundaries.

You've done a playful revision of mythology in your poem sequence, "Usual Devices." Helen sending email to Menelaeus is quite funny. What motivated you to write this?

I like taking another text and working with it in a way that's new. The *Iliad* takes itself seriously; it has to because it's an epic. We can't write epics now, I think, without this sense of irony.

What the twentieth century allows us to do is have this sense of irony. The *Iliad* is fun to work with because it is so serious. It's still one of the texts in the great canon of literature. Probably because I am a woman, I am re-writing it in a feminist way.

So what are the usual devices?

The usual devices have to do with language. I didn't want to call it something like "signs and symbols" — "usual devices" remains kind of neutral. I wanted something neutral.

Your poetry is rich with startling metaphors like "light is an axe through the top of our heads," "a skull is a verb that can't be conjugated." Why is metaphor important to you?

In a way, I think that's where the poet is seeking silence. Though it is almost the opposite when we look at it on a page because we are so aware of language and the tricks that it can do. You could write a metaphor and think, "I'm doing a trick," like jumping through a hoop. I'm thinking of twists of language which cannot be reduced to meaning really easily. Metaphor has this way of jumping. Poets are really good at leaping from one thing to another and putting these things together so you see the world differently.

You are trying to get beyond language with metaphor because we are so constrained by it. We're trying to move into this other place that is not language. You can't lay this out as prose; it's this jump that you are trying to make out there.

You work with silences a lot, gaps, absences. Why does absence fascinate you?

Well, in art you have the sculpture making the form, and then you have the space all around the sculpture. I look at emptiness or absence or forgetting as opposed to memory. At the hearts of the poems I write there is this paradox between memory and forgetfulness, or presence and absence, or what is real and what is unreal. Whenever I bring one of these in, the other is sure to follow.

What is writing, for you?

Freedom. How can I get out of my own traps I have set for myself? Writing is the way out. In poetry you can do *anything you want.* There are endless possibilities.

J. Maureen Hull, Fisher-Poet of Pictou Island

"I'm a Maritimer. I've never lived where I couldn't see the ocean or get to it after a few minutes' walk. The shoreline's the best place to ramble, the place where sea and land and sky meet. The north shore's the best if you want to be solitary; the wharf's where you go to get the news. Interesting things happen at the edge, you soak up the rhythm of the sea, on the boat or on the shore, and those rhythms can't help but find their way into your work. It's not that I couldn't write poetry if I lived away from the shore-line; it's that it would be unimaginably different."

photo: Moira Harding

Maureen Hull was born in Cape Breton and spent most of her life there before leaving to study at Dalhousie University. She has lived on Pictou Island since 1976, where she and her husband fish for a living. Maureen's writing has appeared in numerous journals including The Fiddlehead, Pottersfield Portfolio, Other Voices, Contemporary Verse II, Qwerty, *and* blue shift. *Her poem, "Two Feet Above Sea Level," won the Atlantic Writing Competition (WFNS) in 1995.*

I talked with Maureen in Frenchy's in New Glasgow on a hot August day. Fans billowed skirts and bridal veils around us.

Can you tell me about fishing, and how it fits into your life as a writer?

Fishing is what you do if you want to earn a living here. It's a kind of lifestyle and a whole community that I had no idea existed. I mean, I grew up in industrial Cape Breton and I worked in theatre. From November to April I try to write every day. During the spring, summer and fall, I'm either fishing or running one of my kids back and forth, so I write less often. But it still goes on during the rest of the year.

Is an island an enabling place for you and your creative processes?

Yes. It's wonderful. The only way on and off the island is on this small plane that lands on the road a couple of times a week. It's very private. You can socialize with your neighbours, but you can also disappear for four or five days and not talk to a soul and just write. My kids are older now, so I can indulge myself to incredible lengths. (laughs)

I try to walk every day, up and down the one dirt road, watching the sky and sea, looking for hawks and rabbits, buds and bugs. Wave to my neighbours. And all the while, things are working themselves out in my head. The rhythm of walking sets things in motion, eases the creative process. Sometimes I just have to stop and sit down on the dance-hall steps and scribble some of what's bubbling in my head. When I'm having trouble articulating what I want to say, the best thing to do is go for a walk.

Can living on an island be isolating, too, at times?

Yes. Maybe if I were better at internet stuff, I could probably connect. I'm not too sure... I think I need to look at people's faces when I'm talking about writing. Email or mail is better than not doing it at all, though. I don't see people nearly often enough, and sometimes I really envy my friends in the city who have writers' groups they go to regularly for feedback.

When did you start writing full-time, and why?

I was home-schooling my daughters and grade seven, eight, and nine, they went into correspondence. So I was no longer involved in their education, and that's the point at which I really had the time to do something that had been kind of eating away at me, driving at me — something that I knew I really wanted to do and I finally had the time to do it. This was in about 1991 or 1992.

Can you tell me more about how fishing and writing fit together?

I wrote "Two Feet Above Sea Level" in a boat. I was fishing lobster. All of a sudden, this amazing poem was happening. All day, out in the boat, I'd be thinking about things and parts of it would come. I was thinking, "I'm soaking wet, I can't possibly stop and write anything down." And I'd be out there for six or eight hours and I couldn't write a single word down! What I had to do was, between trawls, keep the parts that really were important, say them over and over in my head and work on the lines. And then I'd come in — and you're really exhausted because you started at four in the morning — eat something, fall into bed and start to scribble and write down as much as I could remember.

Then I'd sleep and get up again. And it happened over quite a long period in the season. Some days it would be new stuff, and some days, lines I had remembered from the day or week before that I wasn't happy with. At the end of the season, I had this whole book full. So that was the start. Since then, I've been writing a lot more poetry.

What things preoccupy you, as a poet?

A lot of it is about where I live, and about fishing. A lot of it is about being connected to the natural world. Recently, a lot of it is about my daughters and where we've come from and the fact that they're moving out into their own lives. I call it domestic poetry. It's about them, and my relation to them.

Why are domestic subjects important to you? — for instance, the family scenes in "Careless" and "The Old House?"

I'm writing about humanity, how we relate, how we fail to relate, connect and misconnect. And I guess it's domestic poetry because the details of where you are support and illuminate relationships, because you are where you come from. So by "domestic," I mean my home surroundings.

You certainly ground your work in the domestic particulars of your world: sliced tomatoes, gin, cinnamon toast, cups that don't match. Your daughters seem to provide an important source of poetic inspiration, too. Is it sometimes difficult to write about things that are so close?

I always have to be aware that there is the privacy issue. There are things I just would not write about in a poem. My daughters are tremendously supportive and encouraging. I'm quite comfortable showing them my work. Sometimes, if something is too corny, they'll say, "much too sentimental, Mom." (laughs)

Who else is your literary community?

I've been sending stories to Shirley Mahood ever since we did that first [Maritime Writers] workshop with Isabel Huggan at UNB. She has always had really good suggestions. Ian [Colford] and Collette [Saunders] are great when I send in submissions [to *Pottersfield Portfolio*], and they are always careful and meticulous. I've gotten very good feedback from *The Fiddlehead,* from Don McKay, when he was there. And I have a friend, Deborah Stiles, who I did the poetry workshop [at UNB] with. Richard Lemm has been very supportive of me.

How is place important to you, as a poet?

Every poem I write is set somewhere in real space, real time. Even if the ideas are abstract, I know clearly what the background was, how the furniture was arranged, what colour the sky was, how things smelled or sounded. There's no question that where I live has had a major impact on my development as a writer. Living in a small, isolated community, working in the fishing industry, surrounded by a community of closely-connected, hard-working, canny, often witty people has given me a solid sense of being grounded in this particular corner of the planet; of being connected with the landscape and the people. There's allowance made here for individuality, even eccentricity. And there's time, especially in the winter, to think and write and pay attention. I try very hard to pay attention to what's around me, to see what's in front of me. Poems take a long time to create, not the actual writing which usually happens very quickly, but the reflection, the slow exploration of an idea. Pictou Island gives me that space and time.

You've also used northern landscapes. I'm thinking of your poem, "Heading North." Do you want to comment on your treatment of the northern landscape because in that poem, you seem critical of the land being exploited for profit?

I went to Tuktoyaktuk for six weeks. I was actually a stowaway. (laughs) There are two different attitudes towards the landscape in that poem. On the one hand, there's the response to the sheer beauty of it. On the other hand, there's the scientific approach to it, all the surveying equipment the male researchers are taking up there. I *was* critical. I wrote the poem recently, but it comes out of memories from before I moved to Pictou Island. I was horrified about what the guys were doing: taking the oil out of the Beaufort Strait and shipping it south. That's why they were there. I suppose it's stronger written from my perspective now, when I'm truly appalled by what they've done up north. If I'd written it then, I think that would have been more muted.

Do you consider yourself an environmentalist?

I hope so. But I feel a lot of guilt because there are a lot of things I should do that I don't. I live in a community where most people are pretty responsible. We had the first recycling depot in Pictou County, and it has been going continuously. Part of it has been imposed on us because it's difficult to get things to Pictou Island. So we tend to recycle more. The lifestyle lends itself to gardening. We all have to provide our own power and water. So you become very conscientious about how much power and water you're using. We're much closer to the repercussions if we screw up. We have only ourselves to blame. I think part of the problem in the rest of the world is that the repercussions are so far away. If your water supply was a closed cycle like it is for us, it would make a difference. As for power, people on Pictou Island have generators, windmills and solar panels.

Let's return to the notion of "domestic archaeology." Archaeology suggests digging, unearthing something. And "domestic" suggests your own particular surroundings. Is that what writing poetry is, for you?

There is a kind of digging that goes on, but not right away. Something wonderful happens, something catches you, a feeling, vision, detail, and it connects with your creative centre, and this poem begins to happen. And then afterwards, when I'm thinking about it, then I really start to think, "What is this really about?" And I've only learned to dig around in the last few years, to dig for that original impetus, where it came from. It's like trying to understand the messages I've been given. Trying to understand myself. A good poem is one where you learn something. You think you're in control, then you realize there's a lot more going on than you were in control of.

Some of your poems seem to try to come to terms with your daughters growing up. Is there a sense of loss being expressed?

"Loss" has a negative connotation. But I suppose there's a bit of loss because you're losing this stage of your relationship, and you've been happy with that. You're saying good-bye to that, but at the same time, wonderful things are going to happen in the future. You're still going to have a relationship, but it will have changed. You're always saying good-bye a little bit. But it's exciting that things keep evolving.

You've expressed the hopeful, positive side of evolving relationships in "Amy and Moira," in the image of the mud from your daughter's boot springing into seed and flower, the future. In some poems, you are looking into the past. In "Domestic Archeology," for example, the speaker is "[hanging] the laundry on the line/with [her] mother's hands." How important is the past, to you?

Rhythms and cycles repeat, and you find yourself in a cycle you remember from your mother's life. That's what that one's about.

Your poems sometimes contain the words "knowledge" and "know." In "Rum Toddy on the Backstep," you write, "knowing / everything is more than I can imagine." What kind of knowledge do your poems impart, for you?

They allow me to explore ideas. Not all of what I'm writing comes out of my conscious mind. There is sometimes information there that I can later retrieve, that I didn't know I had, or that wasn't accessible to me until I wrote about it in a poem. Then I could look at it and think about what it meant. I've always wanted to know everything. (laughs)

Where do want to go as a poet? What do you want to do?

I want to get better. The more I write, the more critical I get. I can do better if I just keep paying attention and growing and learning more. A fair bit of my work has been published, and I'm at the point where I'm wanting to shape it into a manuscript. I can see where some of it belongs together. I'm always afraid of getting lazy, so I make myself do things, write in a certain way. I wrote sonnets for awhile. The best one I wrote was about duct tape. (laughs)

Rescuing Eve:
Regina Coupar and Feminine Spirituality

"Many women are wondering about spirituality. In a Christian context, they are wondering if the voice they hear is really the voice of the Holy Spirit. It is, but they've been told that this voice is something else. So the voice they hear is not acknowledged as such. Part of how I see my job as an artist is to help people affirm those voices from within — not the ones coming from the priest or people on the outside."

photo: Jennifer Coupar

Regina Coupar grew up in Bible Hill, Nova Scotia. She attended the Atlantic School of Theology and Mount Saint Vincent University. A visual artist, writer, teacher, and mother of three, she currently splits her time between Truro and Chester Basin. Regina's visual art, which has been exhibited throughout Nova Scotia and beyond, includes watercolours, oil paintings, stone lithographs, pastels and drawings. Regina's books, published under the Gamaliel imprint, combine her poetry and visual imagery. These books include: The Spirit Sings: Reflections from an Artist's Journal *(Gamaliel, 1992);* Echoes of the Remnant *(Gamaliel, 1993);* Light Among the Shadows: Releasing Feminine Spirit *(Gamaliel, 1995).*

Regina and I talked at her studio in Truro.

You've become a feminist theologian. What is your church background?

I was baptized into the Anglican Church as an infant. When I was very young, my parents moved to Bible Hill, right across the street from a United Church, so my childhood was spent as a regular attendee of the United Church. When I got married, I switched back to Anglicanism. Recently, I've made the decision not to participate actively in the Church. But I'm still a Christian. They're not going to get rid of me that easily. (laughs)

What do you think the problem is?

I think basically the problem is the patriarchal approach we still accept within the Church. While I don't see God as being either male or female, I think as long as the Church is uncomfortable using the pronoun "she" in relation to God, it shows we still harbor patriarchal beliefs.

How do your visual art and your writing relate to one another?

They overlap. When I'm thinking about something, I have a reaction to it. The reaction might be visual. If it's visual, it might be a lithograph, or a watercolour or a drawing. I don't know which medium beforehand. I don't decide; I let it tell me. If it's written, it might be a poem, it might be prose. I try to let it tell me. That's how I think I do my best work. I might look at something today and see a picture. I might look at the same thing tomorrow and hear words I want to write.

Is there such a thing as feminist spirituality?

This is my passion at present. I have been gradually becoming aware of how my sense of spirituality is different from mainline Christian thinking. I've also become aware of how it's different even from mystical women of the Middle Ages. Their visions and words were cloaked in patriarchy, but mine don't have to be. Given their life and their times, that's the way it was. I'm still a Christian, but I don't have to use that kind of language anymore. I'm sure there is a feminist spirituality, but is there one that can also be called Christian? That is my struggle right now. This is a beginning for me, to see if it's possible to reconcile my spirituality with my Christianity.

How does this struggle relate to finding your centre, your sense of identity?

This relates to my thinking about the emergence of a true self. The tree of life means, for me, being connected with my roots. For example, I've known my whole life that my grandmother was Acadian, but all of a sudden this fact became important to me. For me, this parallels a need to know my mythological roots as a Christian. "Eve" is a concept I love, but in Christian terms Eve is not someone to be proud of. The fall is all Eve's fault. The fall is a patriarchal cover-up; I want to rescue Eve.

In terms of Christianity, your work offers some fairly iconoclastic images. In your collage, "Sophia Rising" for example, there is a ripped up Bible, a torn picture of Jesus. Have you come under fire?

I had a two-person exhibition with another woman artist. We took our work to a local gallery and left it there. We came back to the opening later that night and discovered that some of my work had been assembled in a make-shift room set apart from the rest of the gallery. The other artist's images were all over the main part of the gallery. I had brought a small clay sculpture of a woman lying on her back, giving birth to a snake. You can imagine what that would look like, right? The opening was very tense. The reporter who reviewed the show noticed this right away and zeroed in on it. The gallery had been afraid that the work might offend some "church." At that time, I was a student at the Atlantic School of Theology. I was terribly hurt.

You've started your own publishing imprint, Gamaliel, in Truro. Why did you decide to go that route?

I decided to do this because I did a lot of public speaking in church communities and things like that. Some people suggested I work on a book, so I did. I sent it to a publisher and it came back with a lovely rejection letter, which I added to my rejection letters from stories, exhibitions and such. My mother and I were pulling a print in my studio in Bible Hill when the letter from the publisher arrived, and she said, "You can do it yourself." She knew not to say anything else; my mother knows me. (laughs) And about two hours later, it became "my" idea. I had to become a marketing person and a publisher and all these other things — in addition to being an artist and writer.

What's the most difficult aspect of being your own publisher, distributor, and everything else?

Burnout. At the end of writing a book, I didn't really want to talk about it anymore. I wanted to move on to something else. But in order for me to do justice to what I had already done, and to communicate with people, I had to go back "there."

You've written about recovering from the trauma of the rib. Is "rescuing Eve" part of recovering from that trauma?

Yeah. I was recently invited to a Mi'kmaw sweatlodge. I also have some Mi'kmaw blood in my veins. In my paintings, you can see some of that kind of imagery. I was invited to this sweatlodge, but I couldn't participate because I was having my period. I felt "unclean," rejected and disappointed, but they were telling me that I was clean, that if I were to sweat with other women, I, not they, would be defiled! I was not feeling honoured because of the patriarchal tradition I've been brought up in — a tradition in which

Eve is cursed. Periods are called "the curse." So I started thinking about all this and it gave me the key to understanding the problems of Eve. I started thinking about other women I can rescue: for example, Lot's wife.

What do you mean by "rescue?"

It was the realization that having my period was a blessing and not a curse that did it for me. Sometimes when I speak with groups, especially women's groups, part of what I feel my job is, is to affirm what's already there. Many women are wondering about spirituality. In a Christian context, they are wondering if the voice they hear is really the voice of the Holy Spirit. It is, but they've been told that this voice is something else. And so the voice they hear is not acknowledged as such. Part of how I see my job as an artist is to help people affirm those voices from within — not the ones coming from the priest or people on the outside.

You often write about finding your centre, as an artist and a woman. How do you come to have such a strong sense of your own center?

For me, it's a matter of unpeeling other stuff; the centre is always there. It's genuine; it's the most original thing in the world. But it becomes coloured by culture and conditioning and peer pressure. In order to get to it we need to separate what is authentically our own from what we have inherited and borrowed from others. How did I find out that I don't like this? Was it my husband's idea or my own? Slowly, we start to peel all that away. As we do, we are left with the kernel that is really our self. This is our centre; it's original because we are the only one who can really stand in this place.

Deirdre Dwyer, Curiouser & Curiouser

"The whole process of writing is exploratory. When I write the first line, I don't know what's going to come next. Poetry is the unexpected. You see things in a whole new way because the context is different."

photo: Eleonore Schönmaier

Deirdre Dwyer grew up in Musquodoboit Harbour on the eastern shore of Nova Scotia. She studied philosophy at Dalhousie University and English and creative writing at the University of Windsor. Deirdre taught English in Japan from 1987 to 1990. Her first collection of poems is The Breath That Lightens the Body *(Beach Holme, 1999). She has also written* Going to the Eye Stone, *and is at work on her third poetry manuscript,* Theoretical Chocolate. *Deirdre teaches writing in Halifax.*

Deirdre and I talked at the Lord Nelson Hotel in Halifax.

When did you first become interested in reading poetry?

In high school, I read a poem by Gwendolyn MacEwan called "Meditations of a Seamstress." I could relate because I was doing sewing at the time. So poetry was about something I knew, all of a sudden. On the other hand, MacEwan made it a mythical world. I started mostly by reading Canadian women poets: P.K. Page, Margaret Atwood. I don't think I heard of Elizabeth Bishop until later.

When did you begin to write poetry?

In grade five or six. I did haikus for a long time. I never knew I would one day go to Japan. (laughs) I still really like the haiku's brevity, the striking image. In grade twelve, I started writing longer things, reading more. My first published poems were when I was in high school; the poems were in a Halifax magazine called *Mackerel Sky.*

You have travelled pretty extensively throughout southeast Asia. Did you keep journals?

I wrote while I was travelling. When you're in new places, your senses are enriched. To convey that to other people is quite a challenge, and to avoid the stereotypes that belong to those places. The essence of poetry is to capture an experience and translate it so that other people can understand it. But everything has to distil.

But isn't travel disorienting in some ways, too? How does that impact on your writing, that sense of being "out of place"?

It humbles you. You realize that you're not all-important.

You refer, in one of your poems, to a state of mind called "poet-think." When you're in "poet-think," do you see the world differently?

Poets are using metaphors and similes to describe things, so there is that sort of heightening of language. That poem, "The Calling," was about an encounter — with a deer. I was rushing to a reading, and there was suddenly this young deer. It was strange to slow down all of a sudden and communicate with it.

You've written in other poems about unexpected encounters, encounters with an "other." That's a bit like travel, too, isn't it?

That's right. Poetry is the unexpected. You see things in a whole new way because the context is different.

Why is that element of shock or surprise important to you?

You learn things from that sudden revelation. About yourself and the rest of the world.

One of your groups of poems is entitled "Going to the Eye Stone." What is the eye stone?

I read about the eye stone in *Cape Breton Magazine.* They don't know exactly what it is, but think it may be the tip of a conch shell. People who are injured — men who have been working with wood and who have splinters in their eye — have to go to where the eye stone is. They put the stone in the eye. It travels around the eye, finds the splinter, and when they take the stone out, the splinter is gone. So it's a metaphor for healing, a journey. Art is like that. Creativity is one way of healing.

The "eye" seems important to you. Sometimes your poems move into an almost childlike perspective. In "When Sleep Comes," your elegy for Henry DeEll and Larry Lamont, there's a sense of shock, then a shift into a childlike perspective.

Yes, that poem does move into a childlike perspective. Because we want a story, like a child does. There's a sense of security, continuity. Story keeps us going. But in that poem, the story is gone; the story ends abruptly. And children see the world fresh. Seeing the world the way they do is kind of what writing is. And I think there is a strong narrative element in my poems. People want to hear a story. They want to be grounded in something. Sometimes I think people don't read poetry because they think it's going to be "all in the air" — concepts like love, freedom. But as a writer, I want to be grounded, too, by using the senses. I do that through the image; I think visually.

So what comes first for you, when you write, the image or the narrative thread?

Sometimes the thread. I have a new poem called "Sleepover" about going to a friend's overnight, as a child, and how that was disorienting.

Is travel something like returning to childhood? I mean, is the gaze of the traveller somehow childlike? Everything is new, unexpected. Is travel like that for you?

It is. We get so much information about travel, through guides. But the richest experiences are when you're completely surprised. But I don't have to be travelling all the time to be writing. I'm always going back to childhood. And the everyday things that happen can be just as disorienting, surprising. Just looking at nature closely is completely surprising.

How is the Atlantic milieu, natural or cultural, important to you?

Place is very important. It's our connection to nature that feeds us, gives us that sense of surprise. There's a whole mythology connected to place, too. When we were children, going to Blomidon, we were read the stories of Glooscap. And I felt privileged to be in that place; it felt like a spiritual place.

What do you do when you're in exotic places where you don't know the language? I'm thinking of Thailand and other exotic places in your poems. How do you get the story?

You make up your stories. In Thailand, I made up this story about palm trees as earrings for elephants.

I guess then you are freed up to inject a streak of surrealism, if you want? I'm thinking of the lines "A Turkish car wants to eat you, nibbles at your hem." Is that grounded, too, in concrete experience?

Yes, but because I was writing a poem about a skirt, I didn't want to say "I'm writing a poem about a skirt." I become more removed from the poem because it's a relationship between a car and a skirt. The skirt was wounded by the car. So that poem talks about the vulnerability of travel. I don't want always to be the centre of my poems.

You use many questions in your poems. Why?

The world confirms that I don't know everything. The whole process of writing is exploratory. When I write the first line, I don't know what's going to come next.

So it's curiosity that drives you?

Yes. Enigmatic things.

Aren't the questions a way of interacting, too? A way of being "dialogic," having a dialogue?

I would agree with that.

In some of your poems, you are the centre; it's your story. In those poems, what is the function of the "I?"

The "I" provides a sense of continuity; it pieces together those fragments and patterns which do not fall into a neat narrative pattern.

What do you learn from writing?

I learn what things are bothering me. And I love words.

That is obvious in a poem like "Bark," which is a piling up of metaphors which explore ways to describe the bark of a tree. Is that poem about the complexity of bark, or the complexity of language? What's the impetus driving that piece of writing?

My husband and I were splitting wood. It was the visual image; there were so many beautiful colours in the bark, such variety. To try to contain that in a poem was an interesting challenge. Even the surface of this world, suggested by bark itself, is complex. The surface is full of visual pleasures. And there again, I didn't have to include myself; I could concentrate on the bark.

You've written that "words are possibilities." What kind of possibilities?

Words convey a kind of openness, that anything could happen.

You've also written, in a poem called "Skating Over the Moment," that "There are times when I feel that we are on the verge of something astounding; we can do more than just skate over surfaces." How do you know when you've broken through the surface?

When I feel the pleasure of capturing something I've been searching for. Or seeing something from a different perspective; there are a lot of "buts" in my poems. When I'm writing about something I'm looking at it in different ways. I combine these perspectives to form a synthesis of knowledge.

How do you get your sense of the shape a poetic line takes?

There are a number of considerations. Breath is very important. Also how it looks on a page. Sometimes the last word on a line will surprise the first word on the next line. And it depends on the subject of a poem. If you're tentative about something, you're probably going slower because you're more unsure of yourself. If you're sure about something, there might be more of an abundance of images, more energy that keeps the line longer.

There's a great deal of water in your poems. In "High Tide," water seems to be almost a language of its own. There's an image of wave crests shaped like letters, like w's.

Because I live near the water, I see many different waterscapes, and it seems to me that each day the water is saying something different.

The body seems closely connected to it, too. I'm thinking of your poem "Red Animal," in which the menstrual blood which suddenly appears in the bath water is compared to seaweed. Why was it important to you to write "Red Animal"?

The body and "women's subjects" have been minimized and not explored enough in literature. Why can't we write about them?

Your poems also have animals in them. What is it about animals that intrigues you?

That's part of a growing environmental consciousness — a sense of considerateness. There's not just humans in the world. We don't come first. There are a lot of other stories out there, too, that we don't know.

How do you think your work has evolved over the past few years?

I think in *Theoretical Chocolate*, there's a working towards a more spiritual world. But there's still this greediness. One of the lines is, "I want to taste even theoretical chocolate." And with chocolate, there's this richness that I want to experience.

"Spiritual" in what sense?

The sense that God is in nature, within each of us. Sort of a pagan spirit, perhaps.

What is "theoretical chocolate?"

The common things we think we need are food, shelter, fresh air. But there's a whole longer list that includes chocolate. (laughs) "Theoretical chocolate" is a metaphor.

So there's a hunger. I can get the "chocolate" part, but what about the "theoretical" part?

You can get chocolate from almost anything. So "theoretical" chocolate is the pleasure that is innate in almost anything. The beauty.

E. Alex Pierce: Return of the Native

"Place does take care of you, at one level. I have a place in the community, an old place, and in a way, it doesn't matter who I am because they've already decided. Landscape has language attached to it, and you're deeply embedded in it and you don't even know it."

photo: Cindy French

Ellen Alex Pierce grew up in Liverpool, Nova Scotia. She studied music at Mount Allison University and then went on to work in theatre. She taught movement and mask work at the National Arts Centre (Ottawa) and the Banff Centre for the Arts. She has made collarative works with a number of artists — Sandy Moore, Steve Tittle, George Steeves, Trisha Lamie, Felix Mirbt and most recently with Ljiljana Jovanovic at the Banff Centre for the Arts' Music of Sound Winter Residency. Alex Pierce won The Fiddlehead's *1998 Contest for her poem, "Shelter," and was selected as a finalist for The League of Canadian Poets publication,* Vintage '98. *She was an editor's choice in the* ARC *Poem of the Year Contest. Alex Pierce holds a* MFA *degree from Warren Wilson College, North Carolina (1997). She attended the Banff Centre's Writing Studio in the fall of 1998, where she worked with Don McKay. In November, 1997, she started Saltwater Workshop services for writers. She is currently completing her poetry manuscript,* Vox humana.

In 1981, Alex had a chance to buy her grandmother's house in East Sable River, Nova Scotia, and in 1992, she returned to live there. I talked with Alex on her front porch.

You have returned to your ancestral place. Can you talk about how your grandparents, and this place, are important to you?

We came here every summer. One set of grandparents lived a mile from the other. I should have ended up staying here and making pickles. (laughs) We either stayed at Nanny Lloyd's house or Nanny Pierce's house, and they were different worlds. There was a different ethos. Nobody had money, but this one [the Lloyd house] had more elegant things, lace tablecloths. My grandmother was really upright. The other one [grandmother Pierce] was a midwife. She had twelve children and raised fifteen. So there's a different mythology of each place. My sister and I would walk up this hard clay road in our bare feet, and it felt good. We had a lot of freedom as kids. Although I can speak about it now, it's still not ready to be written about. It has to emerge in the right way. If you write off the top of things, you don't say anything that matters, or that connects to anybody else.

What has returning here meant to you?

Maybe the security of place. I loved going to England when I was twenty and getting away from that. I wasn't Carman Pierce's daughter. When I came back here in my forties to recover from working in a burnout job, suddenly, I was Carman Pierce's daughter. I wrote and wrote and wrote. There is a feeling of being really young, and discovering yourself. It is odd to be so old and so young at the same time. Maybe part of discovery and growth is permission to take a leap, be naïve. I didn't see where the mythological figures came in, at the time. Cassandra, and those people, are like chosen personae, people chosen to tell the story. I used to think I was going to write in a historical way — you know, do the research, make those people real, give them back to the world. But it's not going to come that way; it's going to come in layers.

How do you see this place now, as an adult poet?

I can't see this place the way you can because I've been seeing it since I was little. So I don't know, when I look out here, whether I see the garden I've got here now, or the garden my grandmother had. My seeing has a depth, an overlaying, a reverberation, that I'm not even necessarily aware of. But I must have been in this house before I was born. (laughs) There's a real language that goes along with a landscape that you don't even know you have until you go somewhere else. I spent some time in Saskatchewan, at a writers' retreat. We don't have sloughs or coulees; we have creeks and ponds and little valleys. It goes deeper than that — the way people talk about weather. Things have their language.

Maybe you're writing about this place more than you think. Your poems contain images of return, re-entry into an earlier physical and psychic landscape. You've written, for instance, in "St. Pete's," "I am walking in water like all the summers of my childhood." Doesn't that suggest a re-immersion in both time and space?

That was written in Saskatchewan, in a writers' colony. I was in this farm country which was, in a way, like going back to grandmother's place. People read [the poem] as if it's really water, but I was in a place with no water. I love the fact that you read that as water. To develop as a writer, you develop as a reader. There's a kind of suspended correctness. Why does there have to be a final authority? We have less trouble if it's a painting, and one person sees this and one sees that. There's something about language and the precision of language where one could imagine an argument: did she mean water or did she not? What's wonderful to me as a writer is that you, a reader, knew what I was doing, and I didn't even know. I was just trying to get down the green colours of the fields, that connection of water and that security. I was worried that this piece would just be too pretty, but by the time I'd got to the end, I felt I'd got to some interior place that was worthy of the beginning. It's not that it's not precise; it's a precision of a kind of knowing that wants to get quadruple layers in things, and to echo.

There's a lot of layers in your writing, layers of time and space. There often seems to be more than one landscape going on at one time. "St. Pete's" seems to be a meditation on process, too.

It is. It was like discovering what meditation is in the sense of being in time, but not racing with it, and having these other people around me working out their own destinies. It was like what you read about meditation, but it was really happening, this atmosphere and breathing in, breathing out. Maybe that is closer to how a child lives.

There's a garden in "St. Pete's." It seems to be carefully tended, not a wild garden. Why is the garden positioned in the middle of the poem?

One had to go through the garden to get to the last paragraph. There were the carefully staked gladiolias. Then there was this single hollyhock that was completely bent to the wind. Then I saw these half-wild, half-tamed things. I realized that was the monks. They're not finished; they're working on themselves all the time. The garden was wild and tame.

Some of your writing, like "St. Pete's," is written as poetic prose. How does that kind of writing take its shape? What motivates a certain form, for you, a certain way of writing?

The thought and the syntax meshing together doesn't live within the length of a line. I have a sense of a line. I was also hearing the rhythm of the opening lines of Elizabeth Smart's *By Grand Central*

Station I Sat Down and Wept. I scanned a good portion of that novel for a teaching seminar at the end of my MFA program. I wanted to talk about meter *away* from poetry, and my second motivation was to make sure the Americans heard about Elizabeth Smart. I marked the speech stresses, tried varying line lengths to see if I could find a regular pattern in the prose. I did – a kind of regular irregularity — and besides, English speech falls naturally into an imabic flow. Shakespeare's line is iambic pentameter. I found that at the end of certain sections, there would always be a cluster of stresses, and the stresses emphasized emotional high points. When I write this kind of prose, I'm thinking in blocks of words. I'm not writing the kind of sentence I'd use in an essay. The sentence wants to move downwards — it's more vertical than horizontal. I'm thinking spatially and working to create compression.

How do you learn to write vertically "down" through the layers rather than writing "across" in a causal linear sequence?

Writing "down" has to do a lot with the number of stresses you use in a line, and that in turn influences the line breaks. The vertical "drop" or impetus comes from both of those elements. You could say that a poem responds to gravity — the lines are shorter than in prose. In a prose poem, you feel the pushing against the horizontal expansion of the sentence. The desire to get from A to B. You feel the "drop" of the line in poetry. Sometimes I feel the influence of the Shakespearean line. For most of my earlier life, I worked in the theatre — and that's what turned me on to poetry: the distillation and the compression.

To write "down," you need to get a lot into the line, so that what starts the poem is usually pretty compressed. But you need the linear impulse, too: otherwise you may not make sense to your reader.

Does writing "down" have to do with the way you manipulate syntax? In "Diptych," you've written, for instance, "I cannot anything remember."

Oh, that's the poem that starts "Because I am afraid." The syntax is the voice of the poem. I don't write as "on the edge" as much as that anymore. I used to write so much on the edge that my writing was encoded, often hermetic, and couldn't be grasped. But first I had to understand these "messages to myself." There's something that the syntax can say; I have to allow it. When you're trying to say something that's unsayable, it always comes out a bit undefined, and a bit pushed around, but it's worth it.

You've written about the need to tell, or retell. What do you mean by that?

That has to do with repeating the myth, repeating the story. The impulse to retell ... I'll tell you what cleared that up for me — a book called *The Marriage of Cadmus and Harmony* by Roberto Calasso. Calasso starts with the myth of Europa and the bull, and he tells the story different ways. He weaves the story threads in and out — contrapuntally. There's no index in the book. It's awful! But that keeps you in the complexity, keeps the linear mind from taking over.

The stories of women in particular have been mostly unwritten and have not until recently been revised, retold, rethought. In a new poem I wrote in November, there's a passage, "Because unwritten, they had just to tell it/even to air ..." I'm telling about that in a provisional voice. I put that voice into movement, into dance, into theatre — even clowning. I'm happy that I lived long enough to tell it in poems. (laughs) It kept moving through the different disciplines. So maybe writing in a vertical way has something to do with speaking. I know my writing came from speaking to an audience.

What is the poetic image, for you?

It's a live thing. It's a dream. It's the feeling of hitting something internally — there's a coalescence. It keeps feeding into the mind and out into other people. You're going after a connection. In theatre, you'd have to gesture to make the image real, hold the attention. On the page, it arrives from something so important that you say it in a condensed way. In poetry, there's got to be a rhythmic movement. This takes you past the logical explanation.

You've come to poetry a bit later than some writers. You seem to have skipped the whole stage of writing on the surface —

I came up from under. But I've come to the end of solitude. I didn't even have a dog at first. (laughs)

You've really been developing layers through voice, for example, in your use of parenthesis and italics which suggest different layers of voices. Voices seem to reflect different inner states. Can you talk about your use of voice in "Diptych," for example?

In that poem, it's a child's voice trying to come out. The second line says, "Because I am afraid/of everything" — the bent syntax reflects the state of mind; it's a fearful inner place. Almost like before language.

What is poetry, for you?

Poetry is this struggle to move around in language and go to bottom of it, wrestle with it and speak it again. There's this push that says "tell it again," even if it's just telling it to air. I have to fight my syntax out with myself. As a poet, the real craft is on the vision side. There's a two-headed thing that allows odd syntax, but corrects and edits, too. A poem isn't "about." There's a musicality that will make it sound right, but then it might not be precise. But that's different from bending the syntax to make something work.

How does a sense of place get into writing?

The fact of what's going on in a place is so deeply embedded that a writer might not even talk about the place. But the rhythm comes from walking down those roads, from the background sounds, the speech rhythms of the old people. And they did speak in a very different way. All that memory piles up and piles up and you can get at a little piece of it. You can't get "the answer," but it's worth looking for.

You've written in a poem called "The Snakes Transform in the Woodpile" — *"the final eye looks inward." I get the feeling that's an important line for you, a statement about poetic vision and how it happens.*

It's about the process of transformation, about writing. Some of the writing I do is just about the sound and the sense. This was, at first, a more mimetic poem, the snake splitting a skin (which I had actually found). But then, by waiting, I got one step further than representation, the mimetic. It has something to do with writing, memory. The poem could have been just a poem about the snakes. But something changed for me when I brought in the old woman, the old aunt in her hospital bed. There's a shifting, a confidence. The day I did that moved something for me.

Your poetry manuscript is called Vox humana. *What does the title mean?*

It means the human voice. But it is also the name for an organ stop. There was an organ here in the house, in my grandmother's living room. The *vox humana* sounds kind of reedy. It was supposed to imitate the human voice — and I like the clean, clear sound of the Latin.

Is poetry, for you, the search for a lost place? A lost child? A search for "the voice that is the undersinging, the one we have forgotten?"

It is. Isn't that ironic, because I'm sitting here in my grandmother's house. I certainly don't have to search for landscapes that were bombed, sold, or marched over. Here I am sitting in it, so why would anyone ask me if I'm searching for a lost world? But, yes. I was searching for the lost self, for a new self. I was searching for what the artist was trying to become.

My earlier work was teaching movement, working with actors, with masks. I worked in large, open rooms — rehearsal spaces and performance space. Then (in 1985) I was enclosed in an office in Ottawa at the Canada Council. At the same time, I went through a huge love loss — the one that brings you to your knees — metaphorically. I started work with a Jungian analyst in Montreal. Part of the work was writing my dreams. I needed to contain my energy, to put the anguish somewhere. I did that in journals, in writing. You need to hold the physicality of language in a container. I started writing down my dreams, and it was glorious, an invitation to discover. A poem is like that. That snake poem is a kind of container. It wouldn't be enough to say that one is looking for a lost self because that's too broad a term, but in essence, that's the thing. Finding that authentic place, a place that's secure amidst all the pain. That type of search for archetypal beings goes on in the theatre.

In the spring of 1989, I took some time off to replenish my nervous system. I sold my $450 Renault "Le Car" and went to Greece. I saw tangible evidence of figures and sacred space, things that corresponded to that involvement with archetypal beings that underlies the work of theatre — and of course work on oneself in the Jungian sense. I had no idea that there were goddesses. I started reading mythologically because the Jungian work uses the archetypes of Greek goddesses and gods as almost psychological forms. In the theatre, it made sense because I could deal with Demeter and Persephone sooner than the mother-daughter internally. That began to make links. Then Hecate, the old woman, the crone (part of the Demeter –Persephone story) — she was connecting, probably, with the (Lloyd) grandmother from here. I became obsessed with the old woman and the young girl. The discoveries were happening out of necessity. I needed to find out something, to know something.

Then, much later, in 1992, I came back here [to Nova Scotia] and by then I was writing in a different way (from dreams and journals). I started writing poems in the fall of 1989. I imagine as a narrative — that what went "out" from me — to a theatre audience was forced *in* by the office, the small space, the change in psychic environment. Maybe I was just ready to stop speaking, and write. I should give the discipline of transcribing dreams more credit — dreams are incredibly layered. In a dream, the mind is able to present several realities at once — music can do that — polyphonically present several voices at once — but language can't. That's why there's the layering, the quieter voices coming in italics. I need the notation.

How has your work in theatre impacted on you as a poet?

I fell in love with the theatre in 1964. My mother and I went to England for Shakespeare's quatracentenary. It was like seeing your beloved, and knowing. This happened the summer the old Pierce house was being torn down. I was a piano student, just graduated from Mount Allison. We went to Stratford-on-Avon to see the Royal Shakespeare Company doing the history plays. It was the chorus in *Henry V* that changed me. One person was standing there on the stage, and it was the poetry, and incredible costumes. What moved me was the voice in the body in the dark, speaking the poetry. Something extraordinary happened through the speaking in the space. I don't know what happened in that room; maybe it was the collective unconscious. I remember thinking, "It's a voice speaking, it's a flame in the dark." I was twenty. Theatre is poetry in space connecting to mind, the spoken word in space. But it's something that happens imaginatively when we read, too. I really didn't know that I was going to write. But somehow the thread through was going where it needed to go. My mother wanted to write.

So you've made the transition from theatre to writing. The person on the stage has such an immediate contact with her audience. But what about writing?

Well, there's the reader. I'm satisfied with writing. I don't have the need to make theatre any more. It isn't there.

There's a lot of dramatic intensity in your work; in a way the theatre making is still there. And you're able to bring in gesture, too. Can you talk about the relationship between gesture and word?

Writing doesn't want to replicate gesture. If you say "I ran," are you describing the knee bending, the ball of the foot coming up? But I think the impulse to write gesture comes from the theatre.

What does it mean for you to write about sexual passion, as in your poem "Shelter?"

That's transformative, going through the flesh. "Shelter" came out of an ancient place inside, far back. It's not an event I remember; it was like a piece of music. I could hear it, so I wrote it down. This is a passionate meeting — the "shelter" of being completely accepted by someone.

You've written about the violence inflicted on women — in the myths, for example. How do you incorporate that into your retelling of these stories? I'm thinking of a line in your Anastasia poem: "she is supposed to die." Why is this predetermined? Because the event takes place in an earlier story?

Retelling is also writing. So what is the job of the reteller? It isn't enough for me to go back and say, "Sleeping Beauty isn't going to die when she gets pricked with the spindle." I have to respect what's there and look at it again. You can do a crude rewrite — transform all the "victims," change the ending. But what good does that do you?

One of the beauties of Roberto Calasso's work as a mythographer is that you can't quite tell where he is altering the story (right now) and where other writers might have made changes in the past — especially when the story/myth was handed on from one culture to another. What Calasso does is remind the reader that myth is constantly changing. Each telling is a rewrite. And this brings up the question of what is my job as a writer, a poet? I don't exist in a vacuum — I'm speaking from a past into a future. This is a paradox. I'm important because I'm retelling the story. At the same time, I'm just one more teller in a long line of repetitions. I have a responsibility not to be "politically correct" (for my time) or to paint things over, but to grapple with my sense of the story any way I can, write it down. In other words, just get your work done. To ignore the violence is to ignore something that has been encoded in mythology.

What are you doing right now?

I'm finishing a manuscript — *Vox humana*. And one of the hardest questions is, what do I do with the violence? What do I do with the death? The poet seeks beauty and peace, but some of the ugly places have to be talked about.

Eleonore Schönmaier:
A Conversation Fetched Home

"I collect feathers, shells, pebbles, along with the elements of people's lives; I intermingle all this and the poems I write are the gifts I give back. Poetry is conversation. I create poems in the hope that the word-music and the wilderness symbiotically flourish."

photo: Bruce MacLennan

Eleonore Schönmaier was born in Red Lake, northwestern Ontario and raised in the nearby gold-mine community of Madsen. Her home of geographic choice is Ketch Harbour, Nova Scotia. She is the author of the short story collection Passion Fruit Tea *(Roseway Publishing, 1994) and* Treading Fast Rivers *(Harbinger Poetry Series, Carleton University Press, 1999). Currently she works as the Writing Resource Centre coordinator at Mount Saint Vincent University where she also teaches creative writing.*

My conversation with Eleonore took place in the form of emails between Antigonish and Ketch Harbour.

How do you think growing up in northern Ontario has impacted on your imagination?

As a child in the northwestern Ontario bush I was able to combine sensory experience with the imagination. I spent most of my childhood roaming outdoors. This allowed me to be physically present in a world of textures, tastes and sounds. I learned how to stand still and watch, to watch and wait while that black bear walked slowly across my path; that same sense of stillness, delight and trepidation is what writing poetry evokes.

English was a second language for the majority of the people I knew as a child. I learned to listen to the sounds of many languages, whether it was Italian, Ukrainian, German, Cree, Polish or Ojibwa. Listening to the sounds of language is, of course, an intrinsic part of poetry.

When did you begin writing? Did you write fiction first, or poetry?

I only recently re-discovered my grade two report card where my teacher commented: "Eleonore writes very interesting and well-organized stories." I didn't start defining myself as a writer in response to the cocktail party question, "What do you do?" until my late twenties. In my early twenties I worked as a nurse. When I signed up for my first creative writing class (the same university course that I now teach), I was asked what I had written. I said, "letters and journals" which was enough to get me into the course. I was told to come to class with my armour on. I did less and less nursing and more and more writing. I may have been writing all my life but it took me a long time to find myself as a writer and to trust in my own voice and experience. It would have saved me a lot of grief and time if I had simply known all along that I was a writer. But I don't think I was ready to present my work in a public context in my early twenties. I had to gain some sense of confidence first.

How has moving to Nova Scotia impacted on your writing?

It has allowed me to continue to live surrounded by the natural world and this in turn remains an inherent part of my writing. I live in a very supportive community. No one expects me to have a nine-to-five job. It's acceptable to be a writer.

"Full moon" strikes me as a northern poem. Would you say your poems contain both "northern" and "eastern" landscapes, or is this distinction artificial? Can you talk about the use of landscape in your poems?

Oh, absolutely, my work contains both these landscapes. In my newest poems I am writing narrative responses to landscape-based imagery, essentially the intersection of landscape and emotion. Writing about landscape in a context devoid of people is meaningless for me. If I observe the landscape I am present as part of that landscape. Emotions and stories (the stories of my friends, family and neighbours) emerge from the land.

I'm also interested in exploring emotions in relation to a longing for the vanishing wilderness which is partly what the poem "Conversation" is about.

In "Conversation," the speaker, after references to longing, regret and the past, refers to a "conversation fetched home." What a great line. What is "a conversation fetched home"?

A "conversation fetched home" is the inner dialogue we carry home after a period of time alone, absorbed in the natural world.

This "conversation" can, for at least a brief spell, replace the constant ongoing rumble of our thoughts, our daily worries and concerns. It is what we take home from the wild to be woven into our daily lives, an elusive, ethereal presence or perhaps an emptiness. Our lives are so full that we often need an actual emptiness.

There is a lot of motion in your poems, traveling, swimming. Why is this important to you?

I love swimming and travelling and I do as much of both as I can. My family is scattered about the world and we travel to be together. Last summer we had a reunion and I went swimming with my sister, nieces and mother. And I mean swimming, not just splashing about. My three-year-old niece and my mother have muscles in their arms and shoulders. They are in control of their beautiful, physical bodies. At three and a half my niece is able to swim on her own.

Travel and swimming evoke all the senses. In order to fully experience a different country one has to be observant. Paying attention is essential for a safe return from the far corners of the earth or from the other side of the lake. Without visual and auditory awareness it would be impossible for me to write poetry. As a writer the challenge for me is to let words become a sensory presence in my body.

Your poems make extensive use of water. Why does water fascinate you as a poetic figure or metaphor?

Water represents sensuality, serenity and risk. I believe in life immersion rather than absorbing only second-hand experience. I'm not interested in watching a diver on a television program. I want to feel the flow of water all around me and then transform this into words.

In "What we don't think of packing," the poem's speaker refers to loss as a "currency." I find this fascinating. To what extent do you see yourself as an elegiac poet, in other words, a poet of loss? How is loss a "currency"?

Loss is a currency from a country that no longer exists. We want to share the coins in our pockets but with loss this usually isn't possible. The coins become a weight we carry with us, a cherished weight. If we are lucky, with time we learn to carry loss more gently.

I live in a coastal community. The sea often takes life away, people are washed away. I wrote "The Names We Carry" after a local man in his thirties died while out for an evening walk. "What we don't think of packing" is the poem I wrote after the Swissair 111 crash. I don't seek these events out. It's just that they happened near my community and you can't avoid their impact. A number of my neighbours were involved in the jet crash aftermath. It has had an irrevocable effect on their lives. At night they stand at the end of their driveways and look up at the sky. You never expect so many people to die near your home. And you especially don't anticipate having to sift through the remnants. It really changes your headspace.

To what extent is poetry a way of tapping into the unknown? I'm thinking of lines like "the table set/for the dead/but they dine only/ in our absence from "The Names We Carry." Another way of asking this is, as a poet, what is your relationship to death?

Death is an essential part of life and in a rural setting its daily presence is unavoidable. An urban woman said to me, "You have to leave the city to discover death." I walk every day along the edges of coastal cliffs. I find birds' wings, seal bones. There is not sorrow in these objects but beauty. They are reminders to cherish every moment.

Your poems sometimes portray older women — the "grey-haired women" in "The Glide Path," for example. Why is it important to record women at that point in their lives?

I find that older women, contrary to popular stereotypes, often lead exciting, fulfilled lives. Unfortunately, women of my mother's generation often have had to wait until they were older to fully live their lives, but this I believe is changing. I know women in their sixties, seventies and eighties who continue to be as active as they were when they were younger. They're not running marathons but then they were not running marathons in their thirties either. They were raising children and that is a form of marathon.

What kind of act is writing poetry, for you?

I collect feathers, shells, pebbles, along with the elements of people's lives; I intermingle all this and the poems I write are the gifts I give back. When I write a poem out of someone else's experience I give the poem to that person. For me this is an act of communication and gratitude, gratitude for the images and stories that are present daily in my life.

What do you hope to achieve as a poet?

Conversation and the sensory world are essential for sanity. Poetry is a conversation. I create poems in the hope that word-music and the wilderness symbiotically flourish.

Margaret McLeod, Poet of Hazard and Danger

"I got to a point where linearity didn't express reality for me at all. It's a construct. It seems to me that we circle back; we all seem to hold a lot of different selves at the same time, a lot of different realities. Things are constantly shifting."

Margaret McLeod's work has appeared in numerous journals, including Event, CV2, Fiddlehead, Room of One's Own, *and* Pottersfield Portfolio, *and has been anthologized in* The Windhorse Reader: Choice of Poems '93 *and* Water Studies: New Voices in Maritime Literature. *She won first prize for poetry in the Writers' Federation of New Brunswick Literary Competition in 1993. Margaret is currently completing her first poetry collection with the help of a Creation Grant from the Province of New Brunswick. A member of the Wolf Tree Writers group, she lives in Fredericton.*

I talked with Margaret in Fredericton on her birthday.

Where did you grow up?

I grew up all over the province. My father was a forester. I spent the years from age seven to about sixteen in St. Stephen. I lived in the Mirimachi, in Newcastle. But I lived in New Brunswick all my life. The woods are never far away.

How did your writing evolve?

I won't go back to childhood, but when I started writing in a sustained way, I was about twenty-five or so. I probably wrote mostly short stories for several years, then switched back to poetry. I was involved in a group ... Shari [Andrews] and Heather [Browne Prince] were in it, and Robert Gibbs. They were mostly poets. I found that prose – realism, the way I was writing it then — didn't express how I saw the world anymore. I took a course with Gail Taylor called "Creative Writing and the Self." She taught me some different techniques and the way that I wrote changed quite a lot. It was less controlled, more daring in form and technique as well as subject.

You belong to the Wolf Tree Writers group based in Fredericton. Can you talk about how this group is important to you?

It's given me a place to take my work. Sometimes we write at the group. We might do rapid-writes, and our poems get involved with each other's, are inspired by each other's. The germs of some poems come from rapid-writes done in the group.

You seem to write on the edge a lot, on the border between what's real and what's not, on the border between poetry and prose. Your poem "Ghost Child" reflects this. Why are you interested in this kind of writing?

I got to a point where linearity didn't express reality for me at all. It's a construct. It seems to me that we circle back; we all seem to hold a lot of different selves at the same time, a lot of different realities. Things are constantly shifting. I probably have settled down a little since that, because it's also a place where it's really hard to be in the same world you have to work and live in. But, in a way, it's still not linear.

How do you write in a way that captures that flux, that non-linearity?

Some of the things came out of rapid-writes. The first draft tends to be written almost in a trance state. It's very intense for me. But then they're moved around to juxtapose things, or change tenses. Sometimes things I thought were a couple of different poems will end up together. They're worked really hard.

You also seem, in some poems, to be writing about disorientation. How do you write about that and still keep your reader on track?

That's where revising comes in.

You work with white space, the space around the poem, in interesting ways. What does the white space mean to you?

White space is important. It's also the space between the confusions. Sometimes, when things are too much, there's a breath, and then the rushing on again.

How have people responded to your work at public readings?

I've gotten some funny reactions. Well, not funny. One guy laughed his head off during "Ghost Child." Some people got upset, have left. It's nice to be with the Wolf Tree Writers now. There's some protection in that. People don't seem to get as overwhelmed — I do tend to write about dark things. Some people are fascinated by dark things, some people are afraid of them. That's legitimate, too. They don't want to think about things like child abuse.

You sometimes use conventions of Gothic writing to address the terror of sexual abuse. Probably not very many writers would combine elements the way you do: gothicism, postmodern discontinuity, sexual abuse...?

(laughs) It's a wonder I get through it at all. But I don't just write about sexual abuse. I love ghost stories, Stephen King. I started writing a thesis about women and vampire novels. I'm interested in fantasy; I read millions of fairy tales when I was a kid. Hundreds of Gothic novels, the ones from the seventies, where the woman in the long dress is fleeing across the moor. And TV. For me, the definitive show was "The Night Stalker." In St. Stephen, we got a few American channels.

Surely New Brunswick is not always a Gothic space, for you (laughs)?

No, oh God. Who could live like that? (laughs) I often like to go for nice walks in the sunshine.

In a piece called "Welcome the Monster," there's a lot of significance attached to being fifteen years old. The poem also explores imagination, creative process. What is the monster for you?

Monsters are a metaphor. There's a lot of the monstrous in people's lives. Sometimes creative people are seen as monstrous; the monster is imagination. There's bits of autobiography in it, but also imagination. I remember that fifteen was a really difficult year. You're sort of powerless, but you're not a child anymore. It was a year when I did a lot of writing. I think that was a year when I found myself as a writer. I didn't necessarily maintain that, because being a writer would be a pretty exotic thing in a small town. But part of the reason for the "she" is that it's not me.

What do you do when you're not writing?

I'm an extremely postmodern person. (laughs) I read compulsively. I read anything and everything all the time.

Which poets?

Don Domanski is the first one who comes to mind. There's an intensity, a playing with reality. I only discovered his work recently. I know he's influenced me since then. And, of course, the poets in my group [Wolf Tree Writers]. Also Robert Gibbs, Lorna Crozier, Sue MacLeod.

What do reading and writing give you?

Words can sometimes make order out of chaos. And emotions are sort of chaotic. Writing is one way emotions come right at you, and have to deal with them. We try to impose a linearity on everyday life.

What is the genesis of "Ghost Child?"

That was based on when I was pregnant with my daughter, who is now sixteen. I used to have to drive her father (he worked in construction) to somewhere out of town. It was always really early in the morning, icy, nobody else around. It started from there, thinking of different scenarios. I was always scared doing that.

Why do you like playing with multiple versions? Do you want to avoid one definitive version, or closure?

Yes. But that isn't always reflected in my own reading. I like a good "happily ever after" sometimes. I kind of wish I could do that, but I have a hard time doing that. Endings don't last very long. Things are in a constant state of change.

What are you trying to say about knowledge or authority in "No Wolves, I Tell You?" The "experts" in the poem seem to be ironized...?

That poem looks at who is permitted to know about things. What authority tells us is real, the official version. But there actually *are* no wolves in New Brunswick. (laughs)

As well as the Gothic, you play with the carnivalesque. In the poem "Midway," dedicated to your daughter, you explore the carnival. Why are you interested in that?

My daughter was a technical consultant on the names of the rides, so she told me about it. There's the dark carnival, too; that's an old tradition. The germ of that came from working at the exhibition every year, and coming out late at night. Fairs are strange places at night. Why is it called "midway," I wonder?

Maybe another sort of border space? Carnivals have something of the unreal about them. They're edgy places. You seem to me to be a poet of hazard and danger. What do you think of that? (laughs)

(laughs) I like that. I do see the world as hazard, as a dangerous place, back from my childhood. I see it as a place where things can shift. You have to watch for what's behind you, around you.

In some of your poems, the greatest danger is in the most immediate space around you, in the home and in the family. That must be difficult to write about...?

Yes, it's very painful. Funny, I haven't been very comfortable talking about this for awhile. For awhile, all I could think about was child sexual abuse. I mean, I guess that's basically what you're asking about?

Yes.

Now I feel, actually, less safe talking about it in the climate we're in. There's so much questioning about whether it's real, which is another thing that really interests me — what's real, what isn't real, what really is memory? Right now we're all fascinated with serial killers, things from the outside. But sometimes what's inside a person's home is the scariest thing of all — what happens when you close the door.

About the Editor: Jeanette Lynes

Jeanette Lynes teaches English at St. Francis Xavier University. Her articles on Atlantic-Canadian literature have appeared in *Studies in Canadian Literature; Wascana Review; The River Review* (Maine); *A Sense of Place: Re-Evaluating Regionalism in Canadian and American Writing* (Edited by Riegel and Wyile, University of Alberta Press); and *Canadian Children's Literature*. Jeanette Lynes' first collection of poems is being published by Wolsak and Wynn in 1999.

photo: Bernice MacDonald Photography